Second Chance

BRITANNICA
Mathematics in Context

Data Analysis and Probability

TEACHER'S GUIDE

HOLT, RINEHART AND **WINSTON**

Mathematics in Context is a comprehensive curriculum for the middle grades. It was developed in 1991 through 1997 in collaboration with the Wisconsin Center for Education Research, School of Education, University of Wisconsin-Madison and the Freudenthal Institute at the University of Utrecht, The Netherlands, with the support of the National Science Foundation Grant No. 9054928.

This unit is a new unit prepared as a part of the revision of the curriculum carried out in 2003 through 2005, with the support of the National Science Foundation Grant No. ESI 0137414.

National Science Foundation

Opinions expressed are those of the authors
and not necessarily those of the Foundation.

Bakker, A.; Wijers, M.; and Burrill, G. (2006). *Second chance.* In Wisconsin Center for Education Research & Freudenthal Institute (Eds.), *Mathematics in context.* Chicago: Encyclopædia Britannica, Inc.

The Teacher's Guide for this unit was prepared by David C. Webb, Sarah Ailts, Jill Vettrus, Monica Wijers, and Truus Dekker.

ISBN 0-03-039819-3

2 3 4 5 6 073 09 08 07 06

The *Mathematics in Context* Development Team

Development 2003–2005

Second Chance was developed by Arthur Bakker and Monica Wijers. It was adapted for use in American schools by Gail Burrill.

Wisconsin Center for Education

Research Staff

Thomas A. Romberg
Director

David C. Webb
Coordinator

Gail Burrill
Editorial Coordinator

Margaret A. Pligge
Editorial Coordinator

Project Staff

Sarah Ailts
Beth R. Cole
Erin Hazlett
Teri Hedges
Karen Hoiberg
Carrie Johnson
Jean Krusi
Elaine McGrath

Margaret R. Meyer
Anne Park
Bryna Rappaport
Kathleen A. Steele
Ana C. Stephens
Candace Ulmer
Jill Vettrus

Freudenthal Institute Staff

Jan de Lange
Director

Truus Dekker
Coordinator

Mieke Abels
Content Coordinator

Monica Wijers
Content Coordinator

Arthur Bakker
Peter Boon
Els Feijs
Dédé de Haan
Martin Kindt

Nathalie Kuijpers
Huub Nilwik
Sonia Palha
Nanda Querelle
Martin van Reeuwijk

Cover photo credits: (left) © Creatas; (middle, right) © Getty Images

Illustrations
x (bottom) Jason Millet;**13** Christine McCabe/© Encyclopædia Britannica, Inc;
18 James Alexander; **26** Christine McCabe/© Encyclopædia Britannica, Inc;
27 Michael Nutter/© Encyclopædia Britannica, Inc.; **31** Holly Cooper-Olds;
32 Christine McCabe/ © Encyclopædia Britannica, Inc.; **45** James Alexander

Photographs
x Amos Morgan/PhotoDisc/Getty Images; **xvii, xviii** (bottom center) PhotoDisc/
Getty Images; **2** (top) Mary Stone/HRW; (bottom) © Photodisc/Getty Images;
3 © Comstock, Inc.; **4** John Langford/HRW; **5, 6** Victoria Smith/HRW;
7 Sam Dudgeon/HRW; **10, 12** Victoria Smith/HRW; **15** © Stone/Getty Images;
19 (top) M. Mrayati from M. Mrayati et al., series on Arabic Origins of
Cryptology, Vol. 1, Al-Kindi's Treatise on Cryptanalysis, published by KFCRIS
and KACST, Riyadh, 2003 (ISBN: 9960-890-08-2); **21** © Corbis; **25** Victoria
Smith/HRW; **35** Victoria Smith/HRW; **41** © BananaStock

Contents

Dear Teacher,

Welcome! *Mathematics in Context* is designed to reflect the National Council of Teachers of Mathematics *Principles and Standards for School Mathematics* and the results of decades of classroom-based education research. *Mathematics in Context* was designed according to principles of Realistic Mathematics Education, a Dutch approach to mathematics teaching and learning where mathematical content is grounded in a variety of realistic contexts to promote student engagement and understanding of mathematics. The term *realistic* is meant to convey that the contexts and mathematics can be made "real in your mind." Rather than relying on you to explain and demonstrate generalized definitions, rules, or algorithms, students investigate questions directly related to a particular context and develop mathematical understanding and meaning from that context.

The curriculum encompasses nine units per grade level. This unit is designed to be the fourth in the Data Analysis and Probability strand, but it also lends itself to independent use—to introduce students to experiences that will enrich their understanding of probability.

In addition to the Teacher's Guide and Student Books, *Mathematics in Context* offers the following components that will inform and support your teaching:

- *Teacher Implementation Guide,* **which provides an overview of the complete system and resources for program implementation.**

- *Number Tools* and *Algebra Tools,* **which are blackline master resources that serve as review sheets or practice pages to support the development of basic skills and extend student understanding of concepts developed in Number and Algebra units.**

- *Mathematics in Context Online,* **which is a rich, balanced resource for teachers, students, and parents looking for additional information, activities, tools, and support to further students' mathematical understanding and achievements.**

Thank you for choosing *Mathematics in Context.* We wish you success and inspiration!

Sincerely,

The Mathematics in Context Development Team

Second Chance and the NCTM Principles and Standards for School Mathematics for Grades 6–8

The process standards of Problem Solving, Reasoning and Proof, Communication, Connections, and Representation are addressed across all *Mathematics in Context* units.

In addition, this unit specifically addresses the following PSSM content standards and expectations:

Data Analysis and Probability

In grades 6–8, all students should:

- understand and use appropriate terminology to describe complementary and mutually exclusive events;
- use proportionality and a basic understanding of probability to make and test conjectures about the results of experiments and simulations; and
- compute probabilities for simple compound events, using methods such as organized lists, tree diagrams, and area models.

Number and Operations

In grades 6–8, all students should:

- work flexibly with fractions, decimals, and percents to solve problems.

Geometry

In grades 6–8, all students should:

- use geometric models to represent and explain numerical and algebraic relationships.

Math in the Unit

Prior Knowledge

This unit assumes students have worked through the first unit in the Probability strand, *Take a Chance*. This unit also assumes students know and can do the following:

• understand and use the concept of chance;

• make a tree diagram to model a situation;

• use tree diagrams to count favorable and possible outcomes and formulate chance statements;

• convert between, ratios, fractions, percents, and decimals;

• multiply fractions (addressed in the units *Fraction Times, Reallotment,* and *Facts and Factors*);

• make absolute and relative comparisons (addressed in the unit *Ratios and Rates*); and

• interpret and make (cumulative) frequency tables, bar graphs, and other graphs (addressed in the units *Picturing Numbers, Dealing with Data,* and *Expressions and Formulas*).

Second Chance is the second unit in the Probability strand. It builds on students' preformal notions of chance that they developed in the unit *Take a Chance*. This preformal notion is formalized into a definition of chance as the number of favorable outcomes divided by the total number of possible outcomes. Several methods to list and count all possible outcomes and to find all favorable outcomes are used in this unit. One of these methods is the use of a tree diagram, which was introduced and used in *Take a Chance*.

Over the course of this unit, the tree diagram evolves into a chance tree. In a chance tree, not all of the events connected to the different branches have the same chance of occurring. This is indicated by writing the chances (as percents or fractions) directly on the branches of the tree. For example, the two events "rolling a 1 with a number cube" and "rolling no 1 with a number cube" have different chances of occurring. It is possible to use a chance tree to model and analyze the situation of rolling a number cube three times.

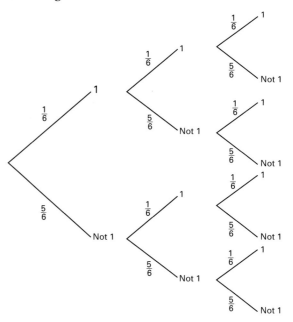

The *theoretical* chances for different outcomes can be calculated without rolling the number cubes. If theoretical chances are not known, statements about chance can be made based on information collected about possible outcomes and how often these occur. The information can be collected by completing an experiment (for example, recording car colors or letters occurring in a text), using a survey (for example, asking people how many days per week they dine together as a family), or completing a simulation (for example, tossing coins a certain number of times). Sometimes, information from the whole population can be collected. More often a sample will be taken. The information can be presented in tables, graphs, or other diagrams. For independent, related events, information is often displayed in a two-way table. The chances that are estimated from this information are called *experimental* chances.

While using two-way tables, students discover that to find the chance for an event to occur, it depends on what you know. For example, if you know a person randomly selected from a sample represented in a two-way table is a man, you use only the information about the men, in the first column, to make chance statements about this person wearing glasses.

	Men	Women	Total
Glasses	32	3	35
No Glasses	56	39	95
Total	88	42	130

Another aspect addressed in this unit is the variability in outcomes of chance experiments and simulations. Experimental chances approach the theoretical chances over many trials.

Students use chance trees as well as the area model to compute chances for combined events. The multiplication rule for finding chances of combined events is addressed through the use of these models. Throughout the unit, students express chances in several ways: as a ratio, a fraction, a decimal, or a percent.

When students have finished this unit, they will:

- understand the meaning of chance or probability;

- express chance for combined event situations using ratios, fractions, decimals, or percents;

- determine all possible outcomes and all favorable outcomes (as a subset of these) for situations with combined events, using tree diagrams and tables;

- use visual models to reason about, estimate, and compute chances;
  - The models used are: tree diagram, chart, table, relative frequency graph, histogram, two-way table, chance tree, and area model.

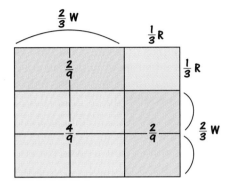

- compute chances;
  - In appropriate situations where all possible outcomes are equally likely, students use the rule: The chance for a certain outcome is the number of favorable outcomes divided by the total number of outcomes.
  - To compute chances for combined (simple compound) events, students use a chance tree or an area model to multiply and add chances.

- use repeated trials in an experiment or simulation to estimate chance (experimental or empirical chance), based on the recorded results;

- compare theoretical and experimental probability;

- understand that in the long run the experimental chance will be close to the theoretical chance; and

- use information from two-way tables to decide whether events are related.
  - This is addressed in this unit at a preformal level. The terms *dependent* and *independent events* are not yet used; they are introduced in the unit *Great Predictions*.

The Data Analysis and Probability Strand: An Overview

One thing is for sure: our lives are full of uncertainty. We are not certain what the weather will be tomorrow or which team will win a game or how accurate a pulse rate really is. Data analysis and probability are ways to help us measure variability and uncertainty. A central feature of both data analysis and probability is that these disciplines help us make numerical conjectures about important questions.

The techniques and tools of data analysis and probability allow us to understand general patterns for a set of outcomes from a given situation such as tossing a coin, but it is important to remember that a given outcome is only part of the larger pattern. Many students initially tend to think of individual cases and events, but gradually they learn to think of all features of data sets and of probabilities as proportions in the long run.

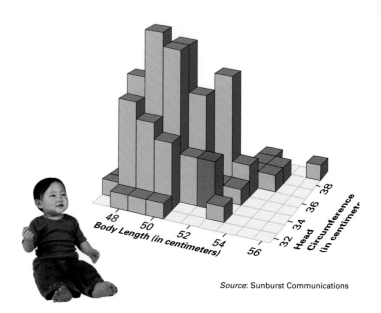

Source: Sunburst Communications

The MiC Approach to Data Analysis and Probability

The Data Analysis and Probability units in MiC emphasize dealing with data, developing an understanding of chance and probability, using probability in situations connected to data analysis, and developing critical thinking skills.

The strand begins with students' intuitive understanding of the data analysis concepts of *most*, *least*, and *middle* in relation to different types of *graphical representations* that show *the distribution of data* and the probability concepts of *fairness* and *chance*. As students gradually formalize these ideas, they use a variety of counting strategies and graphical representations. In the culminating units of this strand, they use formal rules and strategies for calculating probabilities and finding measures of central tendency and spread.

Throughout this development, there is a constant emphasis on interpreting conclusions made by students and suggested in the media or other sources. In order for students to make informed decisions, they must understand how information is collected, represented, and summarized, and they examine conjectures made from the information based on this understanding. They learn about all phases of an investigative cycle, starting with questions, collecting data, analyzing them, and communicating about the conclusions. They are introduced to inference-by-sampling to collect data and reflect on possible sources of bias. They develop notions of random sampling, variation and central tendency, correlation, and regression. Students create, interpret, and reflect on a wide range of graphical representations of data and relate these representations to numerical summaries such as mean, mode, and range.

Organization of the Strand

Statistical reasoning based on data is addressed in all Data Analysis and Probability units. Students' work in these units is organized into two substrands: Data Analysis and Chance. As illustrated in the following map of the strand, the three core units that focus on data analysis are *Picturing Numbers*, *Dealing with Data*, and *Insights into Data*. The two units that focus on probability are *Take a Chance* and *Second Chance*. The sixth core unit in this strand, *Great Predictions*, integrates data analysis and probability.

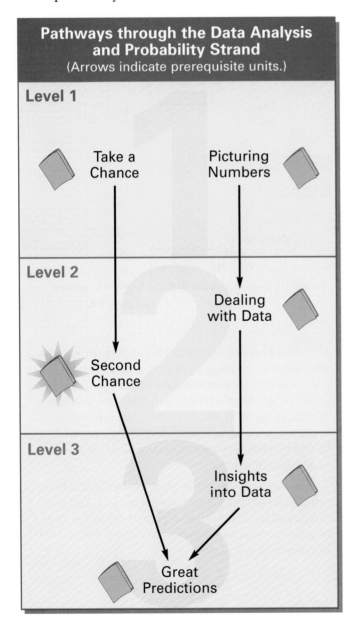

Data Analysis

In the units of the Data Analysis substrand, students collect, depict, describe, and analyze data. Using the statistical tools they develop, they make inferences and draw conclusions based on data sets.

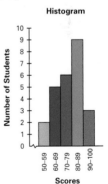

The substrand begins with *Picturing Numbers*. Students collect data and display them in tabular and graphical forms, such as histograms, number line plots, and pie charts. Measures of central tendency, such as the mean, are used informally as students interpret data and make conjectures.

In *Dealing with Data*, students create and interpret scatter plots, box plots, and stem-and-leaf plots, in addition to other graphical representations. The mean, median, mode, range, and quartiles are used to summarize data sets. Students investigate data sets with outliers and make conclusions about the appropriate use of the mean and median.

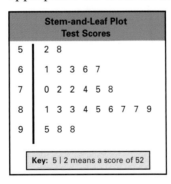

Sampling is addressed across this substrand, but in particular in *Insights into Data*, starting with informal notions of representative samples, randomness, and bias. Students gather data using various sampling techniques and investigate the differences between a survey and a sample. They create a simulation to answer questions about a situation. Students also consider how graphical information can be misleading, and they are introduced informally to the concepts of regression and correlation.

In *Great Predictions*, students learn to recognize the variability in random samples and deepen their understanding of the key statistical concepts of randomness, sample size, and bias. As the capstone unit to the Data Analysis and Probability strand, data and chance concepts and techniques are integrated and used to inform conclusions about data.

Chance

Beginning with the concept of fairness, *Take a Chance* progresses to everyday situations involving chance. Students use coins and number cubes to conduct repeated trials of an experiment. A chance ladder is used as a model throughout the unit to represent the range from impossible to certain and to ground the measure of chance as a number between 0 and 1. Students also use tree diagrams to organize and count, and they use benchmark fractions, ratios, and percents to describe the probability of various outcomes and combinations.

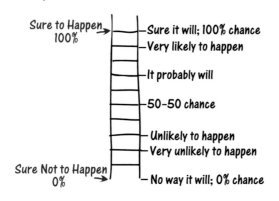

The second probability unit, *Second Chance*, further develops students' understanding of fairness and the quantification of chance. Students make chance statements from data presented in two-way tables and in graphs.

	Men	Women	Total
Glasses	32	3	35
No Glasses	56	39	95
Total	88	42	130

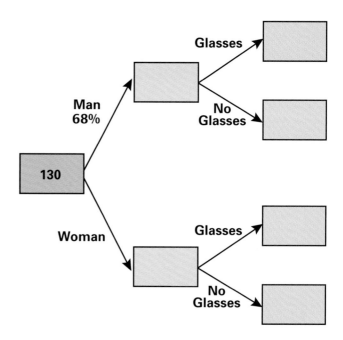

Students also reason about theoretical probability and use chance trees as well as an area model to compute chances for compound events. They use information from surveys, experiments, and simulations to investigate experimental probability. Students also explore probability concepts such as complementary events and dependent and independent events.

These concepts are elaborated further in the final unit of the strand, *Great Predictions*. This last unit develops the concepts of expected value, features of independent and dependent events, and the role of chance in world events.

Critical Reasoning

Critical reasoning about data and chance is a theme that exists in every unit of the Data Analysis and Probability strand. In *Picturing Numbers*, students informally consider factors that influence data collection, such as the wording of questions on a survey, and they compare different graphs of the same data set. They also use statistical data to build arguments for or against environmental policies.

In *Take a Chance*, students use their informal knowledge of fairness and equal chances as they evaluate decision-making strategies.

In *Dealing with Data*, students explore how the graphical representation of a data set influences the conjectures and conclusions that are suggested by the data. They compare advantages and disadvantages of various graphs and explore what you learn from using different measures of central tendency.

Throughout the curriculum, students are asked to view representations critically. Developing a critical attitude is especially promoted in *Insights into Data*, when students analyze graphs from mass media.

In *Second Chance*, students explore the notion of dependency (for instance, the relation of gender and wearing glasses) and analyze statements about probabilities (for instance, about guessing during a test).

In *Great Predictions*, students study unusual samples to decide whether they occurred by chance or for some other reason (pollution, for instance). They explore how expected values and probability can help them make decisions and when this information could be misleading.

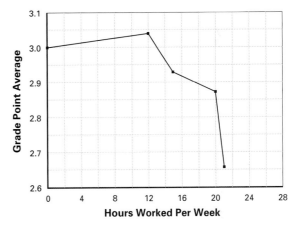

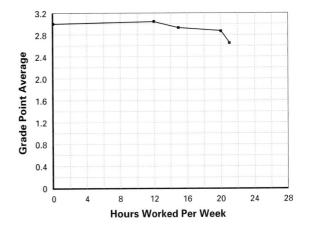

Student Assessment in Mathematics in Context

As recommended by the NCTM *Principles and Standards for School Mathematics* and research on student learning, classroom assessment should be based on evidence drawn from several sources. An assessment plan for a *Mathematics in Context* unit may draw from the following overlapping sources:

- **observation—As students work individually or in groups, watch for evidence of their understanding of the mathematics.**

- **interactive responses—Listen closely to how students respond to your questions and to the responses of other students.**

- **products—Look for clarity and quality of thought in students' solutions to problems completed in class, homework, extensions, projects, quizzes, and tests.**

Assessment Pyramid

When designing a comprehensive assessment program, the assessment tasks used should be distributed across the following three dimensions: mathematics content, levels of reasoning, and difficulty level. The Assessment Pyramid, based on Jan de Lange's theory of assessment, is a model used to suggest how items should be distributed across these three dimensions. Over time, assessment questions should "fill" the pyramid.

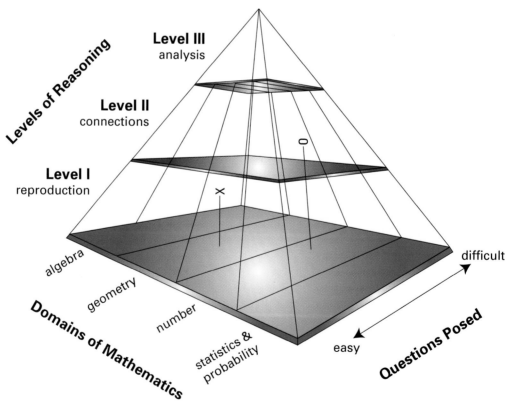

Levels of Reasoning

Level I questions typically address:

- recall of facts and definitions and
- use of technical skills, tools, and standard algorithms.

As shown in the pyramid, Level I questions are not necessarily easy. For example, Level I questions may involve complicated computation problems. In general, Level I questions assess basic knowledge and procedures that may have been emphasized during instruction. The format for this type of question is usually short answer, fill-in, or multiple choice. On a quiz or test, Level I questions closely resemble questions that are regularly found in a given unit substituted with different numbers and/or contexts.

Level II questions require students to:

- integrate information;
- decide which mathematical models or tools to use for a given situation; and
- solve unfamiliar problems in a context, based on the mathematical content of the unit.

Level II questions are typically written to elicit short or extended responses. Students choose their own strategies, use a variety of mathematical models, and explain how they solved a problem.

Level III questions require students to:

- make their own assumptions to solve open-ended problems;
- analyze, interpret, synthesize, reflect; and
- develop one's own strategies or mathematical models.

Level III questions are always open-ended problems. Often, more than one answer is possible and there is a wide variation in reasoning and explanations. There are limitations to the type of Level III problems that students can be reasonably expected to respond to on time-restricted tests.

The instructional decisions a teacher makes as he or she progresses through a unit may influence the level of reasoning required to solve problems. If a method of problem solving required to solve a Level III problem is repeatedly emphasized during instruction, the level of reasoning required to solve a Level II or III problem may be reduced to recall knowledge, or Level I reasoning. A student who does not master a specific algorithm during a unit but solves a problem correctly using his or her own invented strategy may demonstrate higher-level reasoning than a student who memorizes and applies an algorithm.

The "volume" represented by each level of the Assessment Pyramid serves as a guideline for the distribution of problems and use of score points over the three reasoning levels.

These assessment design principles are used throughout *Mathematics in Context*. The Goals and Assessment charts that highlight ongoing assessment opportunities—on pages xvi and xvii of each Teacher's Guide—are organized according to levels of reasoning.

In the Lesson Notes section of the Teacher's Guide, ongoing assessment opportunities are also shown in the Assessment Pyramid icon located at the bottom of the Notes column.

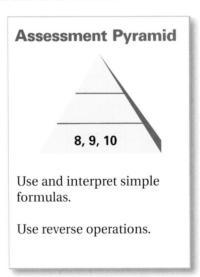

Assessment Pyramid

8, 9, 10

Use and interpret simple formulas.

Use reverse operations.

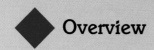

Goals and Assessment

In the *Mathematics in Context* curriculum, unit goals, organized according to levels of reasoning described in the Assessment Pyramid on page xiv, relate to the Strand goals and the NCTM *Principles and Standards for School Mathematics*. The *Mathematics in Context* curriculum is designed to help students demonstrate their understanding of mathematics in  each of the categories listed below. Ongoing assessment opportunities are also indicated on their respective pages throughout the Teacher's Guide by an Assessment Pyramid icon.

It is important to note that the attainment of goals in one category is not a prerequisite to attaining those in another category. In fact, students should progress simultaneously toward several goals in different categories. The Goals and Assessment table is designed to support preparation of an assessment plan.

	Goal	Ongoing Assessment Opportunities		Unit Assessment Opportunities	
Level I: Conceptual and Procedural Knowledge	**1.** Use counting strategies, trees, two-way tables, and rules to find probability.	**Section A** **Section B** **Section D**	p. 3, #6 p. 4, #12a p. 17, #18ab p. 18, #22abc p. 37, #4bd p. 39, #7bc	**Quiz 1** **Quiz 2** **Test**	#3abc #4de #2abc, 3abc, 4c, 5ac
	2. Use different representations (ratios, percents, fractions, and so on) to describe probability.	**Section C** **Section D**	p. 23, #1c p. 28, #9c p. 37, #4c p. 38, #6ab p. 39, #8b	**Quiz 2**	#1, 3a, 4bc
	3. Use complementary probability to determine the chance for an event.	**Section B** **Section C** **Section D**	p. 15, #14ab p. 29, #10b p. 39, #7bc p. 41, #12c	**Test**	#2d
	4. Find the possible outcomes for various situations, games, and experiments.	**Section A** **Section D**	p. 7, #18b p. 39, #7a	**Quiz 1** **Quiz 2** **Test**	#1ab, 4a #1 #1ab, 4abc

	Goal	Ongoing Assessment Opportunities	Unit Assessment Opportunities
Level II: Reasoning, Communicating, Thinking, and Making Connections	**5.** Use simulation and modeling to investigate probability.	**Section B** p. 11, #4abc p. 14, #11b **Section C** p. 29, #10a, 11	**Quiz 1** #4b **Quiz 2** #2, 3c **Test** #4bc
	6. Make decisions using probability and expected values.	**Section C** p. 25, #4abcd p. 26, #6b p. 31, #13b **Section D** p. 37, #4e	**Quiz 2** #3b, 4a
	7. Understand the limitations of and relationship between various models used to find probability.	**Section A** p. 9, For Further Reflection **Section B** p. 20, For Further Reflection **Section D** p. 37, #4a p. 40, #9ab p. 41, #12d	**Quiz 1** #2 **Quiz 2** #2 **Test** #2d, 3d

	Goal	Ongoing Assessment Opportunities	Unit Assessment Opportunities
Level III: Modeling, Generalizing, and Non-Routine Problem Solving	**8.** Understand that variability is inherent in any probability situation.	**Section C** p. 24, #2c	**Quiz 2** #3c
	9. Develop a critical attitude toward the use of probability.	**Section A** p. 6, #16a	**Quiz 1** #1c **Test** #5b
	10. Recognize how probability can be applied in real world situations.	**Section B** p. 13, #8	

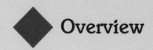
Materials Preparation

The following items are the necessary materials and resources to be used by the teacher and students throughout the unit. For further details, see the Section Overviews and the Materials section at the top of the Hints and Comments column on each teacher page. Note: Some contexts and problems can be enhanced through the use of optional materials. These optional materials are listed in the corresponding Hints and Comments column.

Student Resources

Quantities listed are per student.
- Letter to the Family
- Student Activity Sheets 1–5

Teacher Resources

No resources required

Student Materials

Quantities listed are per student, unless otherwise noted.
- Coin or two-colored disk (same type for each student)
- Copies of parts of newspaper articles or texts from books (one copy with about 25 words per student)
- Large sheets of paper (per pair of students)
- Two different colored number cubes (two for each student)
- Ruler
- Thumbtacks (one per pair of students)
- Toothpicks (per pair of students)

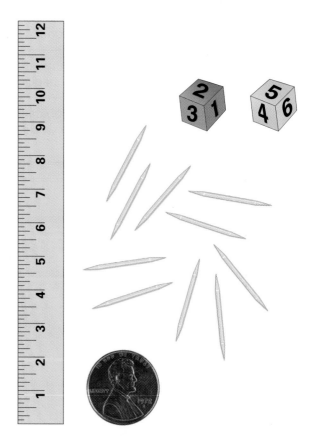

BRITANNICA

Mathematics
in
Context

Student
Material
and
Teaching
Notes

◆ Contents

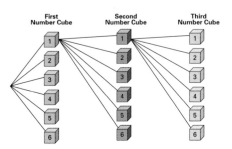

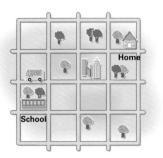

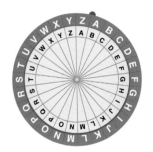

Dear Student

One thing is for sure: Our lives are full of uncertainty. We are not certain what the weather tomorrow will be or if we are going to win a game. Perhaps the game is not even fair!

In this unit you learn to count possibilities in smart ways and to do experiments about chance. You will also simulate and compute chances. What is the chance that a family with four children has four girls? How likely is it that the next child in the family will be another girl? You will learn to adjust the scoring for games to make them fair.

Sometimes information from surveys can be recorded in tables and used to make chance statements.

Chance is one way to help us measure uncertainty. Chance plays a role in decisions that we make and what we do in our lives! It is important to understand how chance works!

We hope you enjoy the unit!

Sincerely,

The Mathematics in Context Development Team

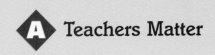

Section Focus

Students investigate situations in which several choices need to be combined like choosing pants, a T-shirt, and shoes for a possible outfit. They use tree diagrams, tables, ordered lists, and smart calculations to find the total number of possible outcomes. They also reason about the theoretical chances for outcomes, which can be found by applying the following rule:

$$\text{Chance} = \frac{\text{Number of favorable outcomes}}{\text{Total number of possible outcomes}}$$

Pacing and Planning

Day 1: Make a Choice		Student pages 1–3
INTRODUCTION	Problems 1 and 2	Describe and evaluate methods for counting combinations of outfits.
CLASSWORK	Problems 3–5c	Find the number of possible outfits and make and use a tree diagram.
HOMEWORK	Problems 5d and 6	Find the number of possible trips a class can take using a tree diagram.

Day 2: Families		Student pages 3–5
INTRODUCTION	Problem 7	Reason about the chances for having one boy and two girls.
CLASSWORK	Problems 8–11	Use tree diagrams to find possible outcomes and probabilities.
HOMEWORK	Problems 12 and 13	Write chance statements and reason about the probability of having all boys in a family with three children.

Day 3: Families (Continued)		Student pages 5–7
INTRODUCTION	Review homework.	Review homework from Day 2.
ACTIVITY	Activity, page 5	Complete a chance activity involving two number cubes and find a way to list all possible outcomes.
CLASSWORK	Problems 14–16	Find possible combinations and reason about the chance for certain sums when two number cubes are rolled.
HOMEWORK	Problems 17 and 18	Reason about the number of outcomes and probabilities when rolling number cubes.

Day 4. Codes		Student pages 7–9
INTRODUCTION	Review homework.	Review homework from Day 3.
CLASSWORK	Problems 19 and 20	Find the chance to correctly guess a four-digit locker combination.
HOMEWORK	Check Your Work For Further Reflection	Student self-assessment: Find the probability of events for various situations.

Additional Resources: Additional Practice, Section A, Student Book page 45

Materials

Student Resources

Quantities listed are per student.

- Letter to the Family
- **Student Activity Sheets 1** and **2**

Teachers Resources

No resources required

Student Materials

Quantities listed are per student.

- Two different colored number cubes (two for each student)

* See Hints and Comments for optional materials.

Learning Lines

Theoretical Chance

In this section, a formal rule to find theoretical chances on outcomes is presented. Chance is defined as:

$$\frac{\text{Number of favorable outcomes}}{\text{Total number of possible outcomes}}$$

Students use this rule in several situations, such as in the situation of finding the chance that a three-child family will have three boys. Note: the assumption is made that the chance of having a boy or a girl are equal, which is not quite true if you study the statistics on births.

Chances are written as ratios, fractions, or percents and sometimes as decimals. Decimals are mostly only used as an in between result when converting ratios or fractions to percents.

Models

The tree diagram that was introduced in the unit Take a Chance is used in this section to model and structure several situations involving combined events (like choosing an outfit, or rolling two number cubes) or a sequence of events (like having three children).

Students use this model to count possible and favorable outcomes. Later in the unit, in Section D, the tree diagram is transformed into a chance tree. In addition to the tree diagram, a table is used as a model to structure and list all possible outcomes. This is done to model the outcomes for rolling two number cubes, since a tree diagram would have become 36 endpoints and be rather cumbersome.

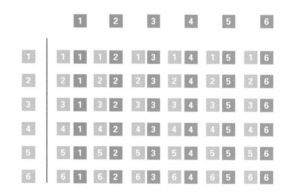

At the End of the Section: Learning Outcomes

To find chances, students can use the rule:

$$\text{Chance} = \frac{\text{Number of favorable outcomes}}{\text{Total number of possible outcomes}}$$

They are able to use several models to structure and model situations involving different outcomes.

 Make a Choice

Make a Choice

Here are Robert's clothes.

1 Have students discuss possible "smart ways" to count the number of outfits. Have them share their strategies and make sure all outcomes are listed.

3a Students should explain why each statement is true or false.

3b Students can check each other's statements.

1. How many different outfits can Robert wear to school? Find a smart way to count the different outfits.

Hillary says to Robert, "If you pick an outfit without looking, I think the **chance** that you will choose my favorite outfit—the striped shirt, blue pants, and tennis shoes—is one out of eight!"

2. Is Hillary right? Explain why or why not.

3. **a.** Which of the statements Robert makes about choosing his clothes are true?

   i "If I choose an outfit without looking, the chance that I pick a combination with my striped shirt in it is four out of 16."

   ii "If I choose an outfit without looking, the chance that I pick a combination with my tennis shoes in it is two out of 16."

   iii "If I choose an outfit without looking, the chance that I pick a combination with both my tennis shoes and my striped shirt is one out of eight."

   b. Write a statement like the ones above that Robert might make about choosing his clothes. Your statement should be true and begin with, "If I choose an outfit without looking, the chance that I pick…."

Reaching All Learners

Intervention

If students have difficulty with problem 2, suggest that they use the answer to problem 1 where all 16 outfits were listed. If students did not list the outfits in problem 1, but only gave the total number of outfits, advise them to list each outcome at this time.

Solutions and Samples

1. Robert can wear 16 different outfits.

   Students may list these in different ways. They may draw each of the outfits, describe them, or make a table or use a tree diagram.

   Combinations are:

   Green shirt, brown pants, dress shoes or tennis shoes (2 outfits)

   Green shirt, blue pants, dress shoes or tennis shoes (2 outfits)

   Striped shirt, brown pants, dress shoes or tennis shoes (2 outfits)

   Striped shirt, blue pants, dress shoes or tennis shoes (2 outfits)

   Yellow shirt, brown pants, dress shoes or tennis shoes (2 outfits)

   Yellow shirt, blue pants, dress shoes or tennis shoes (2 outfits)

   Blue shirt, brown pants, dress shoes or tennis shoes (2 outfits)

   Blue shirt, blue pants, dress shoes or tennis shoes (2 outfits)

2. No, Hillary is not right. Sample explanation: Robert can choose from 16 different outfits (see 1). Only one of those is Hillary's favorite, so the chance is one out of 16.

3. a. i. True. There are four outfits out of 16 with the striped shirt.

      ii. False. Half of the outfits have tennis shoes. Two out of 16 is not the same as $\frac{1}{2}$.

      iii. True. Two out of the 16 outfits have both the striped shirt and the tennis shoes. Two out of 16 is the same as one out of eight.

   b. Answers will vary. Sample student work:

      If I choose an outfit without looking, the chance that I pick an outfit without my striped shirt is 12 out of 16.

Hints and Comments

Overview

Students investigate the number of outfits that can be made by combining different items of clothing. They investigate and write chance statements about the probability of choosing different outfits by chance.

About the Mathematics

In the unit *Take a Chance*, students were introduced to several methods for counting possible outcomes: systematic lists, tree diagrams, and tables. Students were also informally introduced to the multiplication strategy to find the number of possible outcomes. In this case, they would need to multiply the number of shirts (4), by the number of pants (2), and by the number of pairs of shoes (2). Students revisit the topic of making different combinations and reason about the chance for different possible outcomes if selected randomly. Chances are expressed as ratios and connected to simple benchmark fractions.

Planning

Students may work on problems 1–3 in small groups. Have a class discussion about the methods students used in problem 1 before proceeding with problems 2 and 3. Discuss students' statements for problem 3b.

Comments About the Solutions

1. This problem was also addressed in the unit *Take a Chance*. Discuss students' methods. If students do not recall using tree diagrams, this is not a problem since they are re-introduced later in this section.

Notes

4a With the additional pair, Robert now has three pairs of pants.

4b Clarify that Robert already bought the pants; that is, the problem should be solved based on 3 pants.

1–4 Be sure to discuss these problems thoroughly before having students work on problem 5.

5a If students are not familiar with tree diagrams from the unit *Take a Chance*, you may want to complete problem 5a as a whole class.

5 List all possible outcomes to show students how to interpret tree diagrams.

 Make a Choice

4. a. How many different outfits can Robert wear if he buys another pair of pants?

   b. If he buys another pair of pants, how does the chance that Robert picks Hillary's favorite outfit (striped shirt, blue pants, and tennis shoes) change? Explain.

A Class Trip

Grade 7 in Robert's school is planning a two-day class trip to a lake for a science field trip.

They can choose to go to one of four lakes: Lake Norma, Lake Ancona, Lake Popo, or Lake Windus.

Besides choosing the lake, the class has to choose whether to camp out in a tent or to stay in a lodge and whether to take a bus tour around the lake or a boat trip.

The class has to make a lot of decisions!

5. a. Finish the **tree diagram** on **Student Activity Sheet 1**. Write the right words next to all the branches in the tree.

   b. **Reflect** How many different class trips are possible for Robert's class to choose?

   c. How does this problem relate to the problem about the different outfits Robert can choose?

   d. How many possibilities are there if Robert's class does not want to go camping?

Reaching All Learners

Accommodation

Have a transparency of **Student Activity Sheet 1** available to help students understand the use of a tree diagram.

Intervention

You may want to make a tree diagram for different "outfit problems" as a class before doing problem 5.

Solutions and Samples

4. a. With an extra pair of pants 8 new different outfits can be made, so this gives a new total of 24 different combinations. This can be seen by extending the answer to problem 1.

b. Now the chance of choosing Hillary's favorite outfit is 1 out of 24, or $\frac{1}{24}$. Sample explanation: There are now 24 different outfits instead of 16, but still only one that Hillary likes best.

5. a.

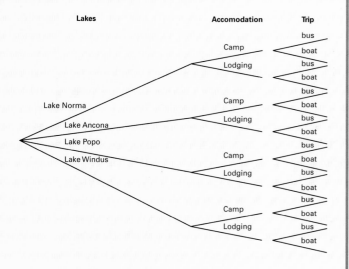

b. 16. The tree ends in 16 branches, where each path to an endpoint of the branch is a different field trip.

c. Both have the same structure and a total of 16 possibilities. The same tree can be used for Robert's outfits: 4 T-shirts (instead of four lakes); two pants (instead of two types of lodging); two types of shoes (instead of two trips on the lake).

d. Eight, because half of the combinations involve camping, and the other half involve staying in a lodge.

Hints and Comments

Materials

Student Activity Sheet 1 (one per student)

Overview

Students find the number of possible outfits for another situation. They make and use a tree diagram to find the possible trips a class can make if they can choose from different places to go, types of lodging, and activities.

About the Mathematics

A tree diagram was introduced in the unit *Take a Chance* as a way to record possible outcomes in multi-event situations, and is re-introduced here. In a tree diagram, each "node" represents a different choice or option, and each branch represents a possible choice. The number of routes or paths towards the branch's endpoints, which is the same as the number of endpoints, is the total number of possible combinations. Each route represents one combination. This leads to the formal introduction of a definition of the chance for a particular outcome as the ratio of "the number of favorable outcomes" to the "number of all possible outcomes." In a tree diagram, every option at each "node" has an equal chance. If this is not the case, a tree diagram cannot be used. Instead, a chance tree, in which the respective chance is written along each branch, should be used. Chance trees are introduced later in this unit in Section D.

Planning

Students may work in small groups on problems 4 and 5, and discuss problem 5b in class.

Comments About the Solutions

5. c. This problem addresses the similarity of the mathematics in problems 1 and 5a. Students should be able to explain why the same "model," or tree diagram, can be used to represent both situations. When using this model, the labels in the diagram need to be adjusted to fit the particular situation.

5. d. This problem informally addresses complementary probabilities. It is stated in a complementary way as "not camping."

A Make a Choice

Notes

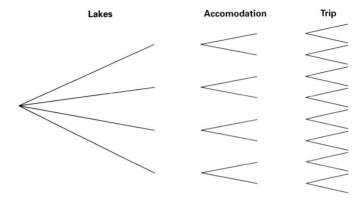

Lakes   Accomodation   Trip

Robert's class finds it hard to decide which trip to choose. Different students like different options. Fiona suggests they should just write each possible trip on a piece of paper, put the pieces in a bag, and pick one of the possible trips from the bag.

6. **a.** If Robert's class picks one of the trips from the bag, what is the chance that they will go camping?

b. What is the chance they will go to Lake Norma?

6 The idea of this simulation may help some students connect chances to a tree diagram. You may want to address the relation between the notes in the bag and where these trips are located on the tree diagram.

7 This type of problem will be revisited in problem 11.

Families

Nearly as many baby girls as baby boys are born. The difference is so small you can say that the chance of having a boy is equal to the chance of having a girl.

Sonya, Matthew, and Sarah are the children of the Jansen family. A new family is moving into the house next to the Jansen house.

They already know that this family has three children about the same ages as Sonya, Matthew, and Sarah. "I hope they have two girls and one boy just like we have," Sonya says, "but I guess there is not much chance that will happen."

7. Do you think the chance that a family with three children where two are girls and one is a boy will move in next door is more or less than 50%? Explain your reasoning.

Assessment Pyramid

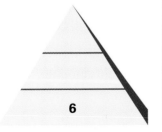

6

Use counting strategies and trees to find probability.

Reaching All Learners

Intervention

You may want to have students complete another example of a chance problem. Ask, How many different sandwiches (with one of each choice) could you make if you can choose from:

- *whole wheat or white bread;*
- *ham, beef, or turkey; and*
- *American or Swiss cheese?*

Solutions and Samples

6. a. The chance they will go camping is 8 out of 16, or $\frac{8}{16}$ or $\frac{1}{2}$, since 8 of the 16 trips in the bag have "camp" on it. This can also be seen in the tree diagram.

  b. The chance they will go to Lake Norma is 4 out of 16, or $\frac{1}{4}$.

7. The chance is less than 50%; it is $\frac{3}{8}$. Explanations will vary.

- Listing all possible combinations for families with three children

  BBB; BBG; BGB; **BGG**; GBB; **GBG; GGB**; GGG, and finding the ones with two girls and a boy, shows that only 3 out of 8 have two girls and one boy. This is less than half.

- Using a tree diagram will also show three out of the eight possibilities have two girls and one boy.

Hints and Comments

Overview

Students find the chance for different combinations of class trips from page 2. They reason about the chance that families with three children have one boy and two girls.

About the Mathematics

In a multi-event situation, there are often several ways in which a particular result may occur. These are called "favorable outcomes." In the example of a family with three children, a combination of two girls and one boy can actually occur in three ways out of the eight possible combinations of three children: BGG, GBG, and GGB. A common mistake is to see the described result ("one boy and two girls") as the only possibility. Students then incorrectly reason: "there are either 0, 1, 2, or 3 boys, so the chance for one boy and two girls is 1 out of 4."

A tree diagram or any other systematic way of recording all of the outcomes can be used to address this mistake by showing all possible and all favorable outcomes. This process was informally addressed in the unit *Take a Chance*.

Planning

Students may work on problem 7 individually or in pairs. Discuss students' explanations for problem 7 in class.

Comments About the Solutions

7. Some students may recall that this context of possible combinations of boys and girls in families was addressed in the unit *Take a Chance*.

A Make a Choice

Notes

8a List all the possibilities. Some students get confused by the triangle on the top of the tree. It is possible to draw the tree without it.

8c and d These are complementary chances. The sum of what *will* happen and what *will not* happen is equal to one (or 100%).

11b In this case, birth order does not matter.

11c Relate this back to problem 7. Do students want to change their answer?

12b Explain that chance statements typically begin with the phrase "The chance that…"

A Make a Choice

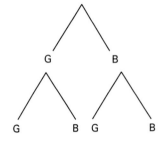

The tree diagram shows different possibilities for a family with two children.

8. a. How many different possibilities are there for a family with two children?

b. Explain the difference between the paths BG and GB.

c. What is the chance that a family with two children will have two girls?

d. What is the chance that the family will not have two girls? How did you find this chance?

You can express a chance as a ratio, "so many out of so many," but you can also use a fraction or a percent. The chance of having two boys in a family with two children is:

one out of four.

This can be written as $\frac{1}{4}$.

This is the same as 25%.

9. Reflect Explain how you can see from the tree diagram that the chance of having two boys is 1 out of 4.

10. Write each of the chances you found in problems 6a, 6b, 8c, and 8d as a ratio, a fraction, and a percent.

11. a. In your notebook, copy the tree diagram from problem 8 and extend it to a family with three children.

b. In your tree diagram, trace all of the paths for families with two girls and one boy.

c. What is the chance that a family with three children will have two girls and one boy? Write the chance as a ratio, as a fraction, and as a percent.

12. a. What is the chance that a family with three children will have three boys?

b. Write another chance statement about a family with three children.

Assessment Pyramid

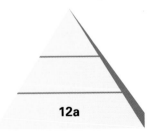

12a

Use trees to find probability.

Reaching All Learners

Intervention

The two-child family problem can be redrawn horizontally like the class trip problem.

Intervention

You may need to review benchmark fractions and percents with students to complete these problems. ($\frac{1}{5} = 20\%$, $\frac{1}{4} = 25\%$, $\frac{1}{3} = 33\frac{1}{3}\%$, and so on.)

Solutions and Samples

8. a. There are four different possibilities. Each "path" in the tree is one possibility.

b. BG means the first child is a boy, the next a girl. GB is the other way around.

c. The chance that a family with two children will have two girls is 1 out of 4, or $\frac{1}{4}$. That's because one of the four routes is GG.

d. The chance that the family will <u>not</u> have two girls is 3 out of 4, or $\frac{3}{4}$. This can be seen in the tree, or students can reason that it is the chance of all possibilities other than the one in 8c.

9. You can see from the tree diagram that the chance of having two boys is 1 out of 4, because there are in total four "paths" or endpoints, and one of the paths has two "B's."

10.

Problem Number	Ratio	Fraction	Percent
6a	8 out of 16	$\frac{8}{16}$ or $\frac{1}{2}$	50%
6b	4 out of 16	$\frac{4}{16}$ or $\frac{1}{4}$	25%
8c	1 out of 4	$\frac{1}{4}$	25%
8d	3 out of 4	$\frac{3}{4}$	75%

11. a.

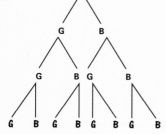

b.

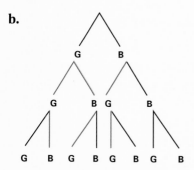

The routes GGB, GBG, and BGG are the paths for families with two girls and one boy.

Hints and Comments

Materials

calculator, optional (one per student)

Overview

Students use tree diagrams to count possible outcomes and find the chances for different outcomes. They express chances as ratios, fractions, and percents.

About the Mathematics

In a tree diagram, each possible outcome can be found by tracing along different paths. To count the total number of outcomes, the paths can be counted, but it is easier to count the endpoints. Several paths can result in the same favorable outcome. The chance for an outcome can be found by dividing the number of favorable outcomes (paths) by the total number of possible outcomes (all paths). This will lead to a formal definition of chance, which is presented on page 5 in the Student Book. Chances can be expressed as a ratio, fraction, percent, or decimal.

Comments About the Solutions

8. b. Students should realize that the order in which children are born sometimes distinguishes possible outcomes and sometimes not, depending on how the problem is stated.

10. You may want to review the relationship among ratios, fractions, and percents.

11. c. You may want to have students use a calculator to change a fraction into a decimal and percent. Another option is to prompt students to recognize that $\frac{3}{8}$ is half of $\frac{3}{4}$.

11. c. The chance is 3 out of 8, which is $\frac{3}{8}$, or 37.5%.

12. a. The chance is 1 out of 8, or 12.5%.

b. Answers will differ. Sample responses:

- The chance of having three boys is the same as the chance that of having three girls, and this is 1 out of 8.
- The chance of having a boy first is $\frac{1}{2}$.
- The chance that a family with three children will have more than one girl is four out of eight, or $\frac{1}{2}$.

A Make a Choice

Notes

13 Suggest using a ratio table. This is called *theoretical probability*.

Activity

Students should share their "systematic way" of making their lists.

14 Ask students how many combinations there are. Have students list the combinations they missed. Remind them that (1, 5) is different from (5, 1).

About 500 families with three children live in East Lynn.

13. Reflect Would you be surprised if 70 of these 500 families with three children had three boys? Explain.

You can often find a chance by calculating:

the number of favorable outcomes

total number of possible outcomes

Number Cubes

Roll two number cubes of different colors 10 times.

List the combination you rolled, like "blue 2 and yellow 5."

Work with three other classmates and list all of your outcomes. Find a systematic way to make your list.

14. Did the four of you roll all possible combinations of the two number cubes? Explain how you decided.

Reaching All Learners

Intervention

Use a smaller number to begin solving problems like problem 13. Example: *If everyone in our class had three children in their family, how many families would you expect to have three boys?* ($\frac{1}{8}$ of 32 students)

Accommodation

Help students set up a chart (or provide copies of a pre-made chart) for the Activity.

Solutions and Samples

13. Answers will vary. Sample answers:

- Based on chance of three boys found in the chance tree, you would expect about $\frac{1}{8}$ of the 500 families to have three boys; this is around 63 families. Seventy is quite close to 63, so this is no surprise; the difference between 70 and 63 is an expected variation.

- Seventy out of 500 is $\frac{7}{50}$; this is about 1 out of 7. The chance of three boys is 1 out of 8; this is not the same but rather close.

14. Answers will vary. Sample answers may include the list students made in the activity with all combinations they rolled. Sample results of 40 rolls in a table:

<table>
<thead>
<tr><th colspan="8" style="text-align:center">Blue</th></tr>
<tr><th></th><th></th><th>1</th><th>2</th><th>3</th><th>4</th><th>5</th><th>6</th></tr>
</thead>
<tbody>
<tr><td rowspan="6">Yellow</td><td>1</td><td>//</td><td>/</td><td></td><td>/</td><td>////</td><td></td></tr>
<tr><td>2</td><td>/</td><td>/</td><td></td><td></td><td>/</td><td>/</td></tr>
<tr><td>3</td><td>//</td><td></td><td></td><td></td><td>//</td><td>/</td></tr>
<tr><td>4</td><td>/</td><td>/</td><td>//</td><td>//</td><td></td><td>/</td></tr>
<tr><td>5</td><td></td><td>///</td><td>///</td><td>/</td><td>/</td><td>//</td></tr>
<tr><td>6</td><td></td><td>/</td><td>///</td><td>/</td><td>/</td><td></td></tr>
</tbody>
</table>

Sample answer:

No, we did not roll all possible outcomes; not all cells of the table have marks in them. For example we did not roll "blue 2, yellow 3."

Hints and Comments

Materials

two different colored number cubes (two for each student)

Overview

Students reason about the variability in outcomes. They complete a chance activity involving two number cubes and try to find a systematic way to list all possible outcomes.

About the Mathematics

Theoretical chances for different outcomes can be found, for example, by making a tree diagram. The tree diagram is a model of the situation. However, there will be variability in the actual outcomes. This is a normal phenomenon and does not mean that something is wrong with the "model." In the example in problem 13, one would expect that about 63 out of 500 three-child-families would have three boys. If it turns out that 70 out of 500 families have three boys, this result would probably be due to "natural" variability in the results.

Planning

Students can work on problem 13 in pairs. Discuss students' explanations in class. For the activity and problem 14, you may want to form groups of four students first and then have each student roll the two number cubes ten times. Discuss the way students listed the outcomes for the activity together in class. After each student has completed this activity, the results for all four students are combined.

Comments About the Solutions

13. If students think it is unlikely that 70 out of the 500 families have three boys, have students share their reasoning. This aspect of variability will be addressed again later in this unit.

14. It is likely that students did not roll all of the possible outcomes. There are 36 different outcomes if colors are taken into account, and four students together rolled the pair of cubes only 40 times. You may want to combine the outcomes from all of the groups to see if all possible outcomes were rolled in class. On page 6, all possible outcomes for rolling two number cubes are listed in a chart.

A Make a Choice

Notes

Give students a few minutes to make the tree diagram for the dice problem. And then ask, *Why is making a tree diagram not a very efficient approach for this type of problem?*

15 Students may wish to write the sums above each combination on **Student Activity Sheet 2**.

16 Be sure students understand why Brenda is incorrect before moving onto the next problem.

You can use tree diagrams to count all possible outcomes of an event. Sometimes you can count all the outcomes by using a chart. For example, if you want to see all possibilities when throwing two number cubes—a blue one and a yellow one—you can use this table.

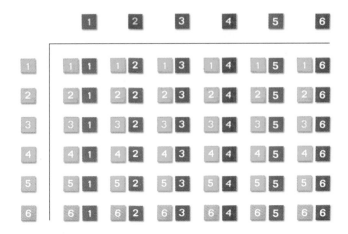

Max rolled two number cubes. On **Student Activity Sheet 2**, you see a circle marking the combination Max rolled.

15. a. What combination did Max roll with the number cubes? What is the sum of the two number cubes he rolled?

   b. Brenda rolled the same sum as Max, but she did not roll the same combination. In the first chart on **Student Activity Sheet 2,** circle all combinations Brenda may have rolled.

   c. In the table at the bottom of **Student Activity Sheet 2,** write the sum for each combination of rolling two number cubes.

Brenda thinks the chance of rolling a sum of eight with two number cubes is the same as the chance of rolling a sum of three. She reasons:

   With two number cubes you can roll a sum of 2, 3, 4, 5, 6, 7, 8, 9, 10, 11, or 12. This makes 11 possibilities in total, so the chance for each of these outcomes is one out of eleven, which is the same as $\frac{1}{11}$, or about 9%.

16. a. Do you agree with Brenda? Why or why not?

   b. Reflect What is the chance that you will roll a sum greater than 8 with two number cubes?

Assessment Pyramid

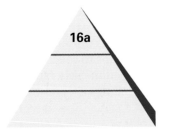

Develop a critical attitude toward the use of probability.

Reaching All Learners

Intervention

Before problem 15, ask students questions about the **Student Activity Sheet 2** chart, such as, *What is the chance of rolling a sum of 4?*

If students have difficulty understanding why Brenda is wrong (in problem 16a), ask them how easy they think it is to roll a sum of 12 compared to rolling a sum of 7, or a sum of 8 compared to a sum of 3.

Hands-On Activity

Students can simulate Max's game and tally the sums they roll.

Solutions and Samples

15. a. Max rolled yellow 4, blue 2; the sum is 4 + 2 = 6

b.

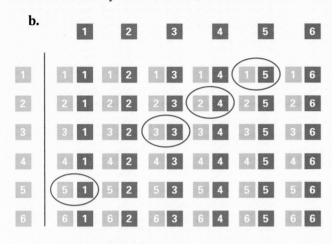

c. Sum of rolling two number cubes

Sum (+)	Blue					
	1	**2**	**3**	**4**	**5**	**6**
Yellow **1**	2	3	4	5	6	7
Yellow **2**	3	4	5	6	7	8
Yellow **3**	4	5	6	7	8	9
Yellow **4**	5	6	7	8	9	10
Yellow **5**	6	7	8	9	10	11
Yellow **6**	7	8	9	10	11	12

16. a. Answers may vary. Sample correct answer:

No, Brenda counts each sum as one possibility, but there are different ways to roll the same sum, so the chance of getting that sum is bigger. For instance, in the table for problem 15c, you can see that there are three ways to roll a sum of four.

b. In the chart or in the table for 15c, these possibilities can be counted. Ten possibilities have a sum greater than eight (see shaded numbers in the chart below).

Sum (+)	Blue					
	1	**2**	**3**	**4**	**5**	**6**
Yellow **1**	2	3	4	5	6	7
Yellow **2**	3	4	5	6	7	8
Yellow **3**	4	5	6	7	8	9
Yellow **4**	5	6	7	8	9	10
Yellow **5**	6	7	8	9	10	11
Yellow **6**	7	8	9	10	11	12

There are 36 different possible outcomes, so the chance you roll a sum greater than eight is 10 out of 36, or $\frac{10}{36}$; this is about 28%.

Hints and Comments

Materials

Student Activity Sheet 2 (one per student)

Overview

In a table, students locate several possible combinations when two number cubes are rolled. They reason about the chance for certain sums when rolling two number cubes.

About the Mathematics

It can be time-consuming to make a tree diagram listing all possible outcomes. For example, a tree for rolling two number cubes would have six branches at the first node, and each of these six branches would split into six more branches at the second node. This would result in a tree with 36 endpoints. If the spacing for the branches is not carefully organized, a tree of this size can become unreadable. In such cases, a table is preferable for presenting all of the possibilities.

When rolling two or more number cubes it is important to note that there is a difference between the outcome of a roll and the sum rolled. Each outcome (such as Black 2, White 3) can be rolled in exactly one way; however, each sum (with the exception of a sum of 2 and 12) can be rolled in a number of ways. A table , such as the one used here for number cubes, can help students distinguish between number of different outcomes and number of different sums. To find chances for each sum, the table can be used to count favorable outcomes. The rule, "chance is the number of favorable outcomes divided by the number of all possible outcomes," can then be used to calculate the chance.

Planning

Have students work on problems 15 and 16 in small groups. Discuss the answer to 16a in class, focusing on students' explanations of Brenda's misconception.

Comments About the Solutions

15. a. You may need to point out to students that by drawing all possible outcomes for the roll of each number cube, it is easier to see the difference between related outcomes such as: Blue 2—Yellow 3 and Blue 3—Yellow 2. This approach also illustrates why different sums differ in the number of ways they can be rolled.

16. b. Some students may reason that a roll of 5 and 6 is the same as a roll of 6 and 5. Refer to the different colors of the number cubes to have students see that these are two different possibilities: Yellow 5—Blue 6 versus Yellow 6—Blue 5.

A Make a Choice

Notes

17. Students must be able to convert ratios to percents to solve this problem.

18b Refer back to the chance situations previously discussed. Use the counting principle to find the total number of outcomes. Example: 4 shirts × 2 pants × 2 shoes = 16 outcomes. Students need to understand this principle before they complete the Codes problem.

19 Discuss this problem before you have students proceed on their own. To prompt student reasoning, you may want to ask, *What are the possible numbers that could work for the third and fourth numbers in the garage code?*

20 Students only need to state that the chance will be much greater.

Jackie says that the chance of rolling a sum of either 9, 10, or 11 with two number cubes is 25%. Tom says, "No, the chance is 9 out of 36."

17. a. Is Jackie right? Explain.

   b. What would you say to Tom?

18. a. Why is a chart like the one shown before problem 15 not useful for listing all possibilities when throwing three number cubes?

   b. What is the total number of possible results when throwing three number cubes? How did you find this?

Codes

You need a code to open some school lockers as well as to access ATM machines and often to open garage doors. A four-digit code is used for the garage door at Brenda's home. The code is made up of numbers from zero to nine. All of the numbers can be used more than once.

For security reasons, if a wrong code is used three times in a row, the garage door will stay locked for the next half hour.

Brenda's brother is at the garage door, but he forgot the code. He only remembers it starts with 3–5, and he knows for sure there is no 0 in the code.

So the code is:

 3   5   —   —   (no zeros)

He decides to guess.

19. a. What is the chance that his first guess is correct?

   b. Suppose the first guess is wrong. He keeps on guessing. How likely do you think it is that he guesses wrong and the door will remain locked for a half hour?

Suppose the code for the garage door consists of four letters instead of four numbers, and Brenda's brother remembers only the first two letters of the code.

20. How will this change the chance that the garage door will remain locked for half an hour?

Assessment Pyramid

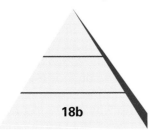

18b

Find the possible outcomes for various situations, games, and experiments.

Reaching All Learners

Intervention

If students are not able to generate any strategies for finding the chance for a correct first guess, you may want to begin listing possible codes for the garage door based on the given information: 3511, 3512, 3513, and so on.

Extension

After completing the Codes problem, discuss the possibilities with your school's lockers. *What is the chance of guessing a correct locker combination with the school lockers?*

Solutions and Samples

17. a. Jackie is right. You can count the favorable possibilities in the chart or table: you can roll a sum of nine in four different ways, a sum of 10 in three different ways, and a sum of 11 in two different ways. So the chance of rolling a sum of 9, 10, or 11 is 9 (i.e., 4 + 3 + 2) out of 36, which is $\frac{9}{36}$, which is $\frac{1}{4}$, or 25%.

   b. Answers will vary. Sample answer:

     Tom is right as well since 9 out of 36 is $\frac{9}{36}$, which is $\frac{1}{4}$, or 25%.

18. a. Since you have only two "sides" in a table, you can only put the outcomes of two number cubes along the left and the top of the table. For three number cubes, you would need an extra direction or dimension.

   b. When rolling three number cubes, there are $6 \times 6 \times 6 = 216$ possible outcomes. This answer can be found in different ways. For each of the 36 possible rolls with two number cubes, you have 6 extra possible outcomes for the third number cube, so 36×6. This can also be found by thinking about the chart as extended in a new direction. You then have a "cube" with $6 \times 6 \times 6$ cells, one for each outcome. Another way to see this is to think about what a tree diagram for rolling three number cubes would look like.

19. a. $\frac{1}{81}$

   Reasoning:

   For the third number in the code, Brenda's brother has 9 possible numbers (1 through 9), and for the last digit he has also nine possible numbers to choose from. So there are $9 \times 9 = 81$ possible ways to finish the code. Only one is correct, so 80 are wrong. So the chance his guess is wrong is $\frac{80}{81}$, which is almost one. So it is almost sure his guess will be wrong.

   b. Very likely. If the first guess was wrong, there are still 80 possible codes to guess; 79 of those are wrong, so the chance of guessing wrong is $\frac{79}{80}$. For the third guess, there are 79 codes of which 78 are wrong. So the chance for guessing wrong three times is very large.

20. The chance of guessing wrong will be even greater because there are more letters (26) than numbers to choose from.

Hints and Comments

Overview

Students continue to investigate the number of possible outcomes and related chances when rolling two or three number cubes. They reason about the chance of guessing a four-digit code for someone who remembered only part of the code.

About the Mathematics

When the chance for a combined event needs to be calculated, the number of possible outcomes for each sub-event (rolling a 9, 10, or 11) can be added together if the events are independent. The chance can then be found using the rule "chance is the number of favorable outcomes divided by the number of all possible outcomes." It is also possible to find the chance for each of the events that make up the combined event and add together the chances. For this example, the combined chance would be: $\frac{4}{36} + \frac{3}{36} + \frac{2}{36}$.

In multi-event situations where there are more than two events, modeling the situation with a table is difficult since a table has just two dimensions, one for each event. A tree diagram can be used, but a large tree is quite cumbersome to make. In that case, the multiplication rule can be used to find the number of all possible outcomes. This rule is informally addressed in this section. Students' prior work with the tree diagram and table in this section leads to the development of the multiplication rule. Have students describe how a tree diagram for a multi-event situation might look without actually drawing it.

Planning

Students may work in small groups on problems 18 through 20.

Comments About the Solutions

18. a. Some students may think of a way to extend the table into the third dimension by making it into a cube.

   b. It may help to think of what a tree diagram for rolling three number cubes would look like. Make a sketch of part of this diagram to help students visualize the beginning of the structure and understand how the number of paths could be calculated. This is an informal introduction of the multiplication rule for finding all possible outcomes for a multi-event situation.

19. a. You may also want to make a sketch of a tree diagram with the possibilities for the third and fourth number.

A Make a Choice

Notes

When discussing the section Summary, ask students to explain how this ratio relates to several of the problems they completed in this section.

For example, when using a tree diagram to find the chance for an event, the number of favorable outcomes was found by counting the branches that matched the event. The number of possible outcomes was found by counting all of the endpoints for the branches.

A Make a Choice

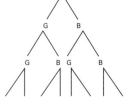

Summary

If you want to count the possible ways that something can occur you can:

- draw all different combinations as you did for Robert's clothes;
- find a smart way to write down all possibilities, such as GG GB BG BB (G for girl, B for boy) for a family with two children;
- use a tree diagram like the one showing the possibilities for the families with three children;
- use a table such as the one for tossing two number cubes;
- use smart calculations as you did for the codes.

If you know all possible outcomes, and you know all outcomes have the same chance of occurring, you can make statements about the chance that certain outcomes may occur. You can do this by counting how many times this outcome occurs compared to all possible outcomes. The chance is:

$$\frac{\text{number of favorable outcomes}}{\text{total number of possible outcomes}}$$

For a family with two children, the four different outcomes GG, GB, BG, and BB are equally likely. Two of those outcomes have a boy and a girl. Therefore, the chance of having a boy and a girl in a family of two children is two out of four, or one out of two.

You can express a chance either as a ratio, like "two out of four;" as a fraction, $\frac{2}{4}$, which is the same as $\frac{1}{2}$; or as a percent, 50%.

Think back to the trip Robert's class is planning.

Reaching All Learners

Extension

Students can make a poster of the Summary with examples of similar situations.

Hints and Comments

Overview

Students read the Summary, which reviews the main concepts covered in this section.

A Make a Choice

Notes

(See page 2.)

> ### Check Your Work
>
> **1. a.** How can you calculate—without drawing a tree diagram—how many possible trips Robert's class can choose? (See page 2.)
>
> Robert says, "The chance we will go on a boat trip is $\frac{8}{16}$."
> Noella says, "I think this chance is 1 out of 2, or 50%."
>
> **b.** Comment on Robert's and Noella's statements.
>
> Mario's advertises, "We serve over 30 different three-course meals." Customers can choose soup or salad as an appetizer; fish, chicken, beef, or a vegetarian dish for the main course; and fruit, ice cream, or pudding for dessert.
>
> **2.** Do you think Mario's advertisement is correct? If yes, show why. If no, give an example of a number of appetizers, main courses, and desserts that will lead to more than 30 different meals.
>
> Diana is having her birthday dinner at Mario's. She decides to make a surprise meal for herself by choosing each of the courses by chance.
>
> **3. a.** What is the chance that Diana has a meal with soup and beef?
>
> **b.** What is the chance that Diana has a meal without fish?
>
> Diana does not like pudding. She thinks the chance that she will pick a meal with pudding for dessert is very small. She says, "The chance that I will pick pudding in my surprise meal is only one out of 24."
>
> **4. a.** Do you agree with Diana? Explain your answer.
>
> **b.** How many meals are possible if pudding cannot be chosen?
>
> ### For Further Reflection
>
> Explain how finding the chance of an outcome using a tree diagram is related to finding the chance using the rule:
>
> $$\text{chance} = \frac{\text{number of favorable outcomes}}{\text{total number of possible outcomes}}$$
>
> You may use an example in your explanation.

For Further Reflection
Reflective questions are meant to summarize and discuss important concepts.

Assessment Pyramid

☐ FFR

1, 2, 3, 4

Assesses Section A Goals

Reaching All Learners

Advanced Learners
Have students use menus from local restaurants to find how many different four-course meals can be served. Students can assume the four courses are appetizers, salads, main course, and dessert.
Menus are often included in the restaurant section of local phone directories.

Intervention

You may want to suggest that students make a tree diagram or an ordered list with all three-course meals to support their problem solving.

Solutions and Samples

Answers to Check Your Work

1. **a.** Without drawing a tree diagram, you could write down all possible class trips, but this would take some time. You can also reason that you can choose any of four lakes, and for each lake you can either choose to camp or to stay in a lodge, so you now have 4 × 2 or 8 possibilities. Each of these 8 possible trips can have either a boat or a bus trip. So now you have 8 × 2 or 16 possible class trips from which to choose. In short, the number of possible trips is 4 × 2 × 2 = 16. It might help to think about the branches in the tree.

   b. Robert is right. In the tree, 8 out of the 16 routes have a boat trip. So the chance is $\frac{8}{16}$. Noella is right as well, because half of the trips have the bus tour, and the other half have the boat tour. So the chance they will go on a boat trip is $\frac{1}{2}$, which is 50%. Of course you can also see that the $\frac{8}{16}$ is equal to $\frac{1}{2}$ and to 50%, so now you know that Noella is right too.

2. No, Mario's advertisement is not correct. To find out how many three-course meals Mario serves, you can, for example, draw a tree diagram – with 2 appetizers, 4 main courses, and 3 desserts from which to choose – and count all possible endpoints.

   Or you can list all of the possible menus.

   You can also reason the way you did for problem 1.

   All these methods will lead to the fact that Mario serves 2 × 4 × 3 = 24 different three-course meals.

   There are many ways to make over 30 different three-course meals. For example, Mario could have one more appetizer, which would make 3 × 4 × 3 = 36 meals.

3. **a.** The chance that Diana has a meal with soup and beef is 3 out of 24 or $\frac{3}{24}$ or $\frac{1}{8}$. You can use a tree to find this by counting the meals with soup and beef. You can also reason about how many different meals have soup and beef. You only have a choice for dessert. So three different meals (one for each dessert) are possibilities with both soup and beef out of the 24 possible meals.

   b. The chance Diana has a meal without fish is $\frac{3}{4}$ or 75%. You can find this answer in different ways. For example, you can find how many meals have fish: that is 1 out 4 because there are 4 main courses. So 3 out of 4 do not have fish.

   You can also use a tree diagram and count all menus without fish, There are 18 out of 24, so the chance is $\frac{18}{24}$, which is $\frac{3}{4}$.

Hints and Comments

Overview

Check Your Work problems are designed for student self-assessment. A student who can answer the questions correctly has understood enough of the concepts taught in the section. Students who have difficulties in answering the questions without help may need extra practice. This section is also useful for parents who want to help their children with their work. Answers to these problems are provided in the Student Book on pages 51 and 52. Have students discuss their answers with classmates.

Planning

After students complete Section A, you may assign as homework problems from the Additional Practice section. These problems can be found on Student Book page 45.

4. **a.** No, Diana is not correct. There are 8 menus that have pudding for dessert out of 24, so the chance that she will pick a meal with pudding for dessert is $\frac{8}{24}$ or $\frac{1}{3}$. You can also reason about desserts only: there are 3 options for dessert, so $\frac{1}{3}$ of all possible three-course meals will have pudding. You can also use the tree diagram and count all meals with pudding.

   b. 16 surprise meals are possible if pudding cannot be chosen for dessert. There are two options left for dessert: fruit and ice cream, so there are now 2 × 4 × 2 = 16 possible meals.

For Further Reflection

Explanations will vary. Sample explanation.

To use the rule,

> *Chance = number of favorable outcomes divided by the total number of possible outcomes,*

you need to find the number of favorable outcomes and the total number of possible outcomes. These numbers can be found by making a tree diagram. The total number of possible outcomes is the total number of endpoints in the tree diagram. The number of favorable outcomes can be found by tracing branches or routes in the tree diagram that lead to a favorable outcome.

Section Focus

Students investigate information collected through surveys, sampling, and experiments. They use relative frequencies of outcomes to make statements about experimental (or empirical) probabilities. These statements are only relevant to future events if the situations are repeatable and do not influence each other. In other words, the events should be independent, and the chance for each outcome should be the same for each future event. With experiments, many trials are often required before the experimental probability approaches the theoretical probability.

Pacing and Planning

Day 5: Car Colors		Student pages 10 and 11
INTRODUCTION	Problems 1 and 2	Reason about the most common car colors.
ACTIVITY	Activity, page 11	Study the results of data collected for car colors and collect data on car colors from a local parking lot.
HOMEWORK	Problems 3 and 4	Graph and analyze data and use findings from data to make "chance statements."

Day 6: A Word Game		Student pages 12–14
INTRODUCTION	Review homework. Problems 5 and 6	Review homework from Day 5 and reason about common letters that are likely to show up for an unknown word.
CLASSWORK	Problems 7 and 8	Guess letter frequencies and compare to actual letter frequency data.
ACTIVITY	Activity, page 14	Record the frequency of letters from a selected text.
HOMEWORK	Problems 9 and 10	Graph the results of letter frequencies for student groups and the whole class.

Day 7: A Word Game (Continued)		Student pages 14–16
INTRODUCTION	Problems 11 and 12	Write chance statements and compare these to the percentages in the letter frequency table.
CLASSWORK	Problems 13 and 14	Solve problems involving complimentary chances.
HOMEWORK	Problems 15 and 16	Investigate the relationship between gender and wearing eyeglasses.

Day 8: Who Wears Glasses? (Continued)		Student pages 17–22
INTRODUCTION	Review homework.	Review homework from Day 7.
CLASSWORK	Problems 17–22	Explore the relationship between grade level and TV use.
HOMEWORK	Check Your Work	Student self-assessment: Find chances using two-way tables for various situations.

Day 9: Summary		Student page 22
INTRODUCTION	Review homework.	Review homework from Day 8.
ASSESSMENT	Quiz 1	Assessment of Section A and B Goals
HOMEWORK	For Further Reflection	Reason about the limitations of two-way tables for more complex situations.

Additional Resources: Additional Practice, Section B, Student Book pages 46 and 47

Materials

Student Resources

Quantities listed are per student.

• **Student Activity Sheets 3a** and **3b**

Teachers' Resources

No resources required

Student Materials

Quantities listed are per student.

• Newspaper articles or texts from books

*See Hints and Comments for optional materials.

Learning Lines

Experimental Chance

In this section, experimental (or empirical) chance is explored. Students investigate several situations in which information is collected to estimate the frequency of the possible outcomes. This information can be presented in frequency tables, bar graphs, or other diagrams. The ratio used to find experimental chance is comparable to the rule for theoretical chance.

The chance of a favorable outcome occurring is:

$$\frac{\textbf{Number of Favorable Outcomes}}{\textbf{Number of All Possible Outcomes}}$$

Students collect data by recording the frequency of letters in a sample English text. They use their data to make statements about the experimental chance of randomly selecting certain letters and compare the results of their own sample to relative frequencies of letters from large-scale sampling.

Related Events

Chances depend on what you know. Two-way tables can be used to determine if two events are dependent. This notion is preformally addressed in this section and formalized in the next probability unit *Great Predictions*.

At the End of the Section: Learning Outcomes

Students know the difference between theoretical and experimental probability. They can complete two-way tables and make chance statements that fit this information. From information in two-way tables, students can decide whether events are "related" (or dependent).

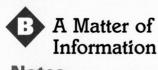
B

A Matter of Information

Car Colors

Sometimes chances can be found because you know and can count all possible results or outcomes. You saw examples of this in Section A.

In other situations, you can make statements about chance by collecting information about the possible outcomes.

Cars come in different colors. Some car colors are more common than others.

1. a. If you go out on the street where you live, what color car do you expect to see most?

 b. Do you think all of your classmates will have the same answer for **a**? Why?

Janet and her sister Karji discuss car colors. Janet says that the favorite color for cars in their neighborhood is white because white cars are easy to see on roads. Karji argues that red is more common because red is a lot of people's favorite color. To find out who is right, Janet and Karji record the colors of 100 cars in a parking lot nearby.

1 Discuss students' answers in class. Make sure they give reasons for their answers. Information on common car colors for certain brands of cars may be found on the Internet.

You may want to ask students what they think of the Janet and Karji strategy for investigating the question about the most common car color.

Reaching All Learners

Extension

To prompt student thinking about issues related to surveys and data collection, complete a quick survey as a class on a topic such as favorite fruit. Use this information to plan what to buy if you were going to have a class "fruit party."

Solutions and Samples

1. a. Answers will vary. Ask students for the reason they named a particular color.

    b. Answers and reasons will vary. Sample answers:

- Probably not. Students have looked at the cars in their own street. It is unlikely that the distribution of colors is the same in every street.

- Perhaps, there are trends in car colors, so cars from the same year may have the same color more often.

Hints and Comments

Overview

Students are introduced to a problem context involving car colors. They reason about the most common car colors and how likely it is that all students will pick the same color as the most common.

About the Mathematics

Chances for outcomes are often predicted from knowledge regarding the number of possible outcomes. Chances that are calculated in this way are referred to as the *theoretical probability*. Theoretical probabilities can be found for regular objects such as number cubes and coins. However, probabilities for situations in the real world often cannot be calculated in this way. In these situations, sometimes data or information is collected to propose statements about the chance for future comparable events. This type of chance is referred to as the *experimental* (or *empirical*) *probability*. That is, the chance statement is based on data collected from an experiment or simulation. In this section, several situations are presented in which experimental probabilities are investigated and used. It is important to note that even when experimental probabilities are used, they cannot predict what will happen next for an individual case. Similar to theoretical probabilities, experimental (or empirical) probabilities give a general idea for the occurrence of outcomes over many trials.

Planning

Have students work individually on problem 1 and then discuss students' answers and the text on page 10 as a whole class.

B A Matter of Information

Notes

2a Make sure to point out that even if the number of white cars recorded was the highest, you still do not know whether this is because of Janet's reason or for some other reason.

Activity

This activity could be assigned to students as homework.

The results are in the table.

2. a. By looking at the results in the table can you tell who is right— Janet or Karji? Explain.

b. Which chance do you think is bigger—that the first car leaving the parking lot is red or that the first car leaving the lot is white? Why?

Color	Number of Cars
Red	13
White	24
Other	63
Total	**100**

Activity

As a class, you are going to investigate car colors in a parking lot or on the street.

First agree on four colors you want to record. Record cars that are not one of those four colors as "other."

Design a form on which you can record the car colors.

Record the colors of 25 different cars. Try to choose a different set of cars from ones chosen by others in your class.

3a Allow plenty of time for this problem. Discuss what type of graph to use. It takes a long time to record class information.

3b Compute the first color as a whole class.

3. a. Combine the class results in one table. Make a graph of the results.

b. Calculate the percentage of cars in each color.

Suppose all of the cars the class tallied in the activity were from the same parking lot.

4. a. Which color car are you most likely to see leaving the parking lot?

b. Is it possible that the first car entering the parking lot the day after you counted colors is a color that you did not record in the activity? Explain your answer.

c. Write three statements involving chance based on your findings about car colors.

Assessment Pyramid

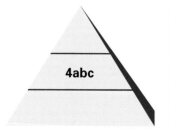

4abc

Use simulation and modeling to investigate probability

Reaching All Learners

Bringing Math Home

After the class agrees on six car colors, assign the Activity for homework so students can complete it with a family member.

Solutions and Samples

2. a. Answers will vary. Sample answers:

- Yes you can see that Janet is correct because there are more white cars (24) than red ones (13) recorded in the table.

- No you cannot tell because you do not know what color the 63 cars were that are counted for "other." Perhaps they are all blue, or more than 24 are blue, and that means that neither Janet nor Karji is correct.

- No, because they have counted only 100 cars, and that is not enough.

- No, because they have only counted on the parking lot, and that is not the same as their neighborhood.

b. Answers will vary. Sample answers:

- If you only look at either red or white, the chance a red car is leaving first may be a little smaller because there are fewer red cars.

- You cannot know, because you don't know which car will be leaving first.

- You cannot tell because if all 63 other cars are blue, the chance that a blue car is leaving first is much bigger.

3. a. and **b.**

The table and the graph will vary; they depend on the data collected in class. Sample student work:

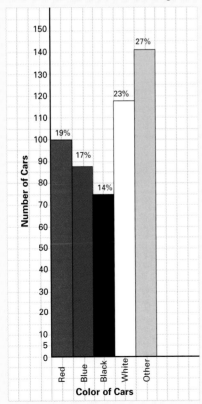

Color of Cars in the School Parking Lot

Color	Frequency	Fraction	Percentage
Red	99	$\frac{99}{519}$	19%
Blue	88	$\frac{88}{519}$	17%
Black	74	$\frac{74}{519}$	14%
White	117	$\frac{117}{519}$	23%
Other	141	$\frac{141}{519}$	27%

Overview

Students study the results of data collected for car colors. Students collect data on car colors from a local parking lot or by observing cars driving down a particular street. Students graph and analyze this data and use their findings to make "chance statements."

See more Hints and Comments on page 79.

4. a. Answers will vary; they depend on the class data set. Sample answers based on sample data set in problem 3:

- It is most likely you see a white car leaving.

- It is most likely you see a car leaving that has a color other than red, blue, black or white.

b. Yes, it is possible that the first car entering the parking lot the day after students counted colors has a color that they did not record as a car color in the activity. This is more likely if the number of colors that are in the table and graph for the class is smaller, that is, if more cars are counted as having "another" unspecified color. The more colors that have been recorded, the less chance this will happen.

c. Statements will vary; they depend on the class data set. Sample students' statements based on the data set for problem 3:

- There is a 99 out of 519 chance the first car leaving the parking lot will be red.

- You are more likely to see white cars leaving than black cars.

- The chance that a car you see leaving is black, blue, or red is 50%.

- The chance you see a car that is not white is $\frac{402}{519}$.

Notes

Discuss familiar game shows in which similar word games are played.

A Word Game

Brittney and Kenji are playing a word game. Brittney is guessing a word that Kenji is thinking about. Kenji makes a row of ten dots, one dot for each letter in the word he has in mind.

Now Brittney has to guess a letter. If the letter is correct, Kenji puts the letter over the correct dot (or dots) in the word. If the letter is not in his word, Kenji writes it down.

Brittney wins if she guesses the correct word before she has guessed eight "wrong" letters. Kenji wins if Brittney guesses eight letters that are **not** in the word and still hasn't guessed his word.

Brittney first asks if the letter E is in the word.

5 If students know the popular word game of "Hangman" or another guessing game involving words, you may want to ask them about their strategies for guessing letters.

   5. Why do you think Brittney first chooses the letter E?

Kenji writes down: . E . . E . . . . E

Brittney tries A, O, I, and U.

Kenji wrote: . E . . E . . A . E   **wrong: O I U**

   6. a. What do you think would be a good letter to ask about next? Why do you think so?

   b. Guess the word or finish the game. (Your teacher has the answer!)

Reaching All Learners

Vocabulary Building

Play "Guess My Word" with math words. Students can be awarded bonus points for defining the word after it has been spelled out.

Solutions and Samples

5. Answers will vary. Sample answers:

- Because E is a common letter.
- Because Kenji thinks there will be an E in the word.

6. **a.** Answers will vary. Most likely students will name a consonant. Sample answers:

- T, because it is a letter that is used in many words.
- Because there will not be many more vowels.

b. The word is: PERCENTAGE

Hints and Comments

Overview

Students investigate a word game and reason about common letters that are likely to show up for an unknown word. This prepares students for the context of letter frequency, which is introduced on the next page.

About the Mathematics

When guessing a word by naming letters (for example, in a game like Hangman), implicit knowledge about common letters will be used by both players. Almost all words have at least one vowel. So a good strategy for guessing is starting with a common vowel. Of course, both players might be familiar with the strategies that are often used, which may cause the player choosing a new word to pick a word with letters that are rarely used, such as Q, Z, and X. The context of letter frequency is investigated further on the next two pages.

Planning

Students can work on problems 5 and 6 individually. You may want to complete problem 6b as a whole class.

Comments About the Solutions

6. b. You can finish this game with your students. They can have five wrong guesses before the game ends. Make letter frequency a topic of discussion. You might refer to the popular game show *Wheel of Fortune* and the strategies contestants use for guessing letters on that show.

Notes

Give students plenty of time to analyze and discuss the table. Ask them what the sum of all the percents should be.

Letter Frequency

Not all languages use the same letters equally often.

7. a. Which letter do you think is used most frequently in the English language?

b. Which letter do you think might occur the least often in the English language?

This table shows the average letter **frequency** in typical written English.

English Letter Frequency			
Letter	%	Letter	%
a	8.17	n	6.75
b	1.49	o	7.51
c	2.78	p	1.93
d	4.25	q	0.10
e	12.70	r	5.99
f	2.23	s	6.33
g	2.02	t	9.06
h	6.09	u	2.76
i	6.97	v	0.98
j	0.15	w	2.36
k	0.77	x	0.15
l	4.03	y	1.97
m	2.41	z	0.07

7c You may want to have students order the letters from this table according to their frequency.

c. How close were your answers for parts **a** and **b**? What are the most and least used letters according to this table?

8. Reflect If you know how frequently letters are used in writing, do you think this will help you when playing the Guess My word game? Why or why not?

Assessment Pyramid

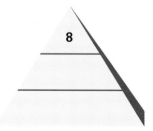

8

Recognize how probability can be applied in real world situations.

Reaching All Learners

Extension

The web page, http://www.simonsingh.net/The_Black_Chamber/frequencyanalysis.html, gives more information about letter frequencies. This website will compute the letter frequencies and produce a bar graph comparing the text entered to the expected frequency for English. Knowledge of letter frequencies can be used to "unlock" secret messages in which the text has been coded by replacing letters with other letters, symbols, or numbers.

Solutions and Samples

7. a. Answers will differ. The **e** and **t** are the most frequently used letters.

b. Answers will vary; the **z, x, j,** and **q** are the letters that occur the least.

c. Answers will vary depending on students answers for parts **a** and **b**. It is likely that students are close. According to the table: **e, t,** and **a** are most frequently used, whereas **z, q, j,** and **x** are the least frequently used.

8. Answers will vary. Sample answers:

- Yes, because you can start asking frequently used letters.

- Yes, because you can pick a word with infrequent letters.

- No, because the person taking the secret word will use a word with very infrequent letters, for example, a word like QUIZ.

Hints and Comments

Overview

Students guess the letter frequencies in the English language and compare this to data in a table for letter frequency.

About the Mathematics

Most people have an idea about which letters are the most and least common in their native language. Frequency tables for many languages are available on the Internet. The table for English on page 13 outlines the average relative frequency for each letter of the alphabet, as they occur in normal English texts. For example, the letter "a" occurs about 8% of the time. Of course, frequencies will vary from text to text, and with the natural evolution of the English language, the average values will shift over time. This table is intended as a general guideline.

The letter frequencies are relative and expressed here as percentages. Since there are 26 letters, the relative frequencies are somewhat small numbers. The highest frequency in the table is for the letter "e," with a frequency of more than 12%. The letters that occur the least have frequencies of around 0.1%. The table is ordered alphabetically and not by frequency.

Planning

Students may work on problems 7 and 8 individually or in small groups. Discuss students' answers to problem 8 in class.

Comments About the Solutions

8. This problem can be looked at from two perspectives: from the person choosing the word or from the person trying to guess the word. They can both make use (explicitly or implicitly) of their knowledge of letter frequencies.

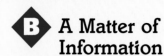
Notes

Activity

If possible, have each pair of students analyze different texts. As they complete their tables, direct students to list letters in alphabetical order. Have one student read the letters while the other student marks tallies on the table.

11ab Some students may require assistance in setting up the class graph. They may want to make a combined frequency table first. Reiterate that students should write three statements.

12 Students should use percents. Be prepared to offer assistance for those students who may need additional practice with fraction, decimal, and percent conversions.

Activity

Take a newspaper article or a text from any book. With a classmate, record the first 100 letters in this text in a frequency table.

9. Use **Student Activity Sheet 3a** to make a graph of the frequencies for each letter.

10. **a.** What is the most common letter in your selection? Was this the same for every pair of students in your class?

    b. Compare your graph with your classmates' graphs. What do you notice?

11. **a.** On **Student Activity Sheet 3b**, combine the letter frequency graphs you made in problem 9 into one class graph.

    b. Write three lines comparing the graph to the letter frequency table.

The results of an experiment or data collection can be used to estimate the chance an event will occur. Chances found this way are called **experimental chances**.

12. Use the data in your frequency table from problem 11 to answer the following:

    a. If you close your eyes and select a letter from a newspaper, estimate the chance that you pick an O.

    b. As a class, compare your answers in part **a** by making a dot plot on the number line of the estimated chances. Use the plot to help you write a sentence about the probability of selecting the letter O from a newspaper with your eyes closed.

    c. Estimate the chance of picking three other letters. Choose one with a high probability of being picked and another with a low probability of being picked. The third one can be any letter you want. Write each answer as a fraction and as a decimal.

Assessment Pyramid

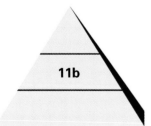

11b

Use simulation and modeling to investigate probability.

Reaching All Learners

Accommodation

Have a tally sheet ready for students to do the newspaper activity. Give students an article with 100 letters blocked off to save time. Have at least six different articles for each class.

Vocabulary Building

Theoretical chance: "what *should* happen"

Experimental chance: "what *does* happen" (This is also known as *empirical probability*.)

Solutions and Samples

9. Answers will vary, depending on students' results. Sample student work for 294 letters.

Letter Frequency from Activity			
Letter	Count	Letter	Count
A	25	N	15
B	10	O	29
C	13	P	5
D	8	Q	1
E	34	R	11
F	6	S	22
G	10	T	23
H	13	U	12
I	16	V	2
J	–	W	2
K	2	X	1
L	16	Y	9
M	9	Z	–

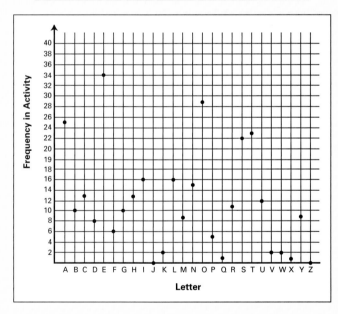

10. **a.** Answer will depend on the results of the activity, sample answer based on the results in problem 9:

   • The most common letter is **e.**

   It is likely that a large number of other pairs of students will also have found the **e** to be the most common letter. This is not sure because a sample of 100 letters is rather small.

Hints and Comments

Materials

newspaper articles or texts from books (one per student);
Student Activity Sheet 3a and **3b** (one per student); overhead transparencies, optional

See more Hints and Comments on page 80.

b. Answers will depend on the results of the activity. It is likely that all graphs will more or less show the same pattern, especially for the most and least common letters.

11. **a.** Answers will vary. The class graph will, in general, show the same pattern as the sample graph shown in the solution for problem 9.

   b Answers will vary, depending on the graph made in part **a**. Sample answers:

   • The letters that are the most common in the graph have the highest percentages in the frequency table as well.

   • The graph and the table show the same kind of pattern of more frequent and less frequent letters; the table shows percentages and the graph absolute numbers.

   • If the results in the graph differ from those in the table, this may be due to the fact that the sample of the texts in class was not representative of all English texts.

12. **a.** Answers will vary, depending on results of the activity. Sample answer based on the table in the solution for problem 9:

   The chance you pick an **o** is 29 out of 294, which is about 10%.

   b. The dot plots will vary. Most likely the chances will be plotted around 7.5% (see frequency table on Student Book page 13). But they can be spread out around this percentage. Sample sentence:

   • The chance of picking the letter **o** is about 8% but can vary between 6% and 10%.

   c. Answers will vary depending on the results of the activity. Sample answers based on the solution for problem 9:

   • The chance of picking an **a** is 25 out of 294; this is $\frac{25}{294}$, which is 0.085, or 8.5%. In the table, this is a high probability.

   • The chance of picking a **z** is 0%. But in reality, this means the chance is very, very small.

   • The chance of picking an **m** is $\frac{9}{294}$, which is 0.03 or 3%.

Section B: A Matter of Information 14T

B A Matter of Information

Notes

You may want to introduce the context and study the table and the graph as part of a whole class discussion.

Family Dining

Instead of collecting information about possible outcomes yourself in order to make chance statements, you often can use information collected by others.

Do students often have dinner with their families? Researchers were interested in answering this question. They surveyed students aged 12 to 17, and the results are in the table below.

Number of Days a Week Children (Age 12–17) Have Dinner with Their Family	Percentage
Don't know	1%
0	5%
1	6%
2	7%
3	11%
4	10%
5	12%
6	7%
7	41%

Source: National Center on Addiction and Substance Abuse

These results can be graphed:

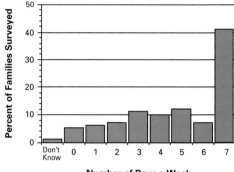

How Often Children Eat Dinner with Family

13a Remind students that more than 5 means 6 or 7.

13b Discuss in class what is meant by the phrase "picked at random": everyone has a chance to be involved.

13c To initiate a discussion of complementary chance, ask, *What percent of the students in this class are girls? How can we use this information to find the percent of boys?*

13. a. If the researchers interviewed 3,000 families, how many reported eating together more than five days a week?

b. If one of the families in the study is picked at random, what is the chance that the family eats together more than five days a week?

c. Use your answer for part **b** to find out what the chance is that a family in the study picked at random eats together five days a week or fewer.

14. a. Is the chance that a family eats together seven days a week greater than, the same as, or less than the chance that they do fewer than five days a week? Explain how you found your answer.

b. What is the chance that a family does not eat together two days a week?

Assessment Pyramid

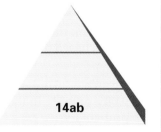

14ab

Use complementary probability to determine the chance for an event.

Reaching All Learners

Intervention

For problem 13a, make sure students understand how to combine events and their respective chances to find the chance for the desired event. For example, less than 5 days a week means 0, 1, 2, 3, or 4 days; the chances can be added.

You may need to break down problem 14a into shorter questions. This would be a good place to introduce inequalities.

Solutions and Samples

13. a. 1,440 families.

In the table (or the graph), you can see 7% eat together six days a week, and 41% eat together seven days a week, so 48% eat together more then five days a week. So if 3,000 families were interviewed, 48% out of 3,000 is 1,440 families.

b. 48%.

This is 7% (eating 6 days a week) + 41% (eating together 7 days a week).

c. 51%.

This is 100% −48% (which is the chance they eat together more than five days a week). This is 52%. Then, subtract the 1% that don't know from 52%. This results in 51% that eat together five days or fewer.

14. a. Greater, since the chance a family in the survey eats together seven days a week is 41%, and the chance they eat together **less** than five days each week is 39%.

The answer can be found in the table by adding up the percentages for 0, 1, 2, 3, and 4 days a week and comparing this to 41%.

b. The chance that a family does not eat together two days a week is 92%. (93% if the "don't know" percentage is added). This answer can most easily be found by subtracting the 7% chance for eating together exactly two days a week from the total of 99% (or 100% if the "don't knows" are counted too). Of course it is also possible to add up all percentages except the 7% for two days.

Hints and Comments

Overview

Students analyze data on family dining. The data presented are for the number of days per week children eat dinner with their family. Students solve problems involving probability, including problems about complimentary chances.

About the Mathematics

Survey data can be used to make statements about how likely certain events are, based on the relative frequencies of results. These statements about chance are reliable for a larger population and for future events only if: a) sample data are selected randomly, b) the sample was large enough and representative of the population, and c) the events are repeatable.

The chances for combined events can be calculated by combining (or adding) relative frequencies. This can only be done only if the events are mutually exclusive (that is, independent). This can be checked by adding the percentages for all events to make sure they add up to 100%. The notion of complementary chance is addressed in the problems on this page.

Planning

Students can work on problems 13 and 14 individually or in pairs.

Comments About the Solutions

13. c. The notion of complementary chances is addressed informally in this problem. It would be useful to discuss the strategy of "subtracting from 100%" at this time. The concept also will be revisited later in this unit.

Notes

Briefly discuss this problem context as a whole class.

Who Wears Glasses?

Some people wear glasses, and some people don't. It is not easy to estimate what the chance is that the first person you meet on the street will be wearing glasses.

Joshua announced that he thinks more men than women wear glasses.

15. **a.** What do you think about Joshua's statement?

   b. How could you figure out whether or not it is true that men are more likely to wear glasses than women?

This illustration was used in an advertisement for an orchestra.

16. Use the illustration to decide whether men or women in the orchestra seem to be more likely to wear glasses. Explain how you came to your conclusion.

16 Make sure students are aware that the number of men and women are not the same.

Reaching All Learners

Intervention

When discussing problem 16, you may find that some students simply counted the number of men and women with glasses, comparing the absolute numbers instead of relative values. This is not a problem at this point in the unit; however, you may still want to illustrate with an example how absolute comparisons can be misleading. Suppose there were 100 men in the orchestra and 33 wore glasses. Also suppose there were 4 women in the orchestra and 3 wore glasses. In this case, more men would be wearing glasses, but a much larger percentage of women would be wearing glasses.

Solutions and Samples

15. a. Answers will vary. Sample answers:

- I agree with Joshua because men are not that much concerned about how they look. Women would rather wear contact lenses than glasses.

- No, because as many men as women have eye problems and will need glasses.

- No, because men play lots of sports, and they need contact lenses to play sports.

b. Answers will vary. Sample response:

You could survey a sample of people and then put your results in a table or a diagram and see if relatively more men or more women wear glasses.

16. Based on the illustration, men seem to be more likely to wear glasses than women. Explanations will vary. Sample explanations:

- There are 32 men wearing glasses, and there are only 3 women wearing glasses.

- About half of the men wear glasses, and only very few of the women.

- 32 out of 88 men wear glasses, and 3 out of 42 women.

- 36% $(\frac{32}{88})$ of the men wear glasses, while only 7% $(\frac{3}{42})$ of the women wear glasses.

Hints and Comments

Overview

Students investigate whether being a man or a woman has any relationship to wearing eyeglasses. This issue is investigated by studying an illustration of members of an orchestra.

About the Mathematics

Students investigate a situation to determine whether two events seem to be related. This is an informal introduction to the notion of dependent and independent events; however, these terms are not yet used explicitly. Students have to think of a way to investigate whether men or women are more likely to wear glasses. They propose a strategy for collecting and organizing the data in order to draw conclusions about whether it is true that men are more likely to wear glasses than women. Students may initially choose to use an absolute comparison of the frequencies instead of a relative one. (Students were formally introduced to relative and absolute comparisons in the unit *Ratios and Rates*.) Using relative frequencies to determine chances in this context is addressed on next page. The concept of dependent and independent events is formalized in the next Probability unit, *Great Predictions*.

Comments About the Solutions

15. b. Students may not realize that they can use ratios (relative frequencies) to find out if wearing glasses is related to gender. This will be addressed explicitly on the next page.

16. The important factor when talking about chance (uncertainty) is the ratio of those with glasses to the total number of men or women. Relative comparison is explicitly addressed in the problems on page 17.

A Matter of
Information

Notes

17 You may want to carefully read this question with students. Be sure students are only counting the men. Ask questions about the chart. *How many men wear glasses?*

Counting men and women with and without glasses can tell you—for those you counted—how many men and women wear glasses. But counting just the number who wear glasses cannot tell you what the chance is that a person wears glasses.

17. Suppose that you randomly select a man from the orchestra. Estimate the chance that this man wears glasses. Explain how you made your estimate.

The **two-way table** summarizes the information about whether or not the musicians in the illustration wear glasses.

	Men	Women	Total
Glasses	32	3	35
No Glasses	56	39	95
Total	88	42	130

A member of the orchestra is chosen at random.

18. a. What is the chance that the person chosen wears glasses?

b. If you were told that the person is a woman, would you change your answer for part **a**?

Chance can be expressed in different ways.

You can express a chance as a ratio, like 35 out of 130.

You can use a fraction, like $\frac{35}{130}$.

You can use decimals or percents such as $\frac{35}{130} \approx 0.269 \approx 27\%$.

Sandra states, "The chance that a randomly chosen woman in the orchestra does not wear glasses is 39 out of 42, which is almost 100%."

Juan states, "I don't agree. The chance that a randomly chosen woman in the orchestra does not wear glasses is 39 out of 130, which is only 30%."

19 This problem offers a great opportunity for a class discussion about two-way tables.

19. a. Explain how Sandra and Juan may have reasoned.

b. Do you agree with Sandra or with Juan? Explain your thinking.

Look at the musicians in the illustration again.

20. How many musicians could you draw glasses on to make it appear that "wearing glasses is as likely for men as for women"?

Assessment Pyramid

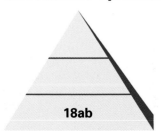

18ab

Use two-way tables to determine probabilities.

Reaching All Learners

Accommodation

Have a transparency of the orchestra available so students can add glasses for problem 20.

Intervention

Write the chance statements using the words: wear glasses/people vs. wear glasses/women.

Hands-On Learning

Use your class as an example of the "orchestra." Count students with glasses. Count boys and girls. Have students make a two-way table from the class data.

Solutions and Samples

17. About 36%.

Explanation: In the orchestra, 32 out of 88 men wear glasses, so if you choose a man at random, the chance he is wearing glasses is $\frac{32}{88} = 0.364$, or 36%.

18. a. The chance that the person wears glasses is 35 out of 130, which is $\frac{35}{130} = 0.27$ or about 27%.

b. Yes. If the person is a woman, you only look at the women. Of the women, 3 out of 42 are wearing glasses. So if you choose a woman at random, the chance she is wearing glasses is only $\frac{3}{42}$, which is about 7%.

19. a. Sandra has looked only at the group of women; 39 out of 42 do not wear glasses. She expressed this as a chance of $\frac{39}{42}$, which is 93% (almost 100%). Juan has compared the group of women without glasses (39) with the whole group (130).

b. Answers may vary. The reasons students give should be discussed. Sample answers:

- I agree with Sandra because if you know the person is a woman, you only need to use information about the women.

- I agree with Juan because I think you should take into account all orchestra members if you want to know the chance of selecting a woman with glasses if you select a person at random.

20. The probability that a man wears glasses is $\frac{32}{88}$, which is about 36%. To ensure that the men and women have equal chances, you could color glasses on 12 more women in addition to the three who already wear glasses. This would make the proportion of women go to $\frac{15}{42}$, which is about 36%.

Hints and Comments

Overview

Students continue their investigation of an illustration of members of an orchestra to find out whether wearing glasses is dependent on being a man or a woman.

About the Mathematics

Organizing information into a two-way table supports the analysis of whether or not two events are related. Relative frequencies can easily be calculated from a two-way table and can be used to make statements about the likelihood of certain events.

Students discover that probabilities can change if you have more information about the situation. In other words, chance statements depend on what you know. If you know, for example, that a randomly selected person from the orchestra is a man, you know the chance of selecting a person wearing glasses is about 36%. If you did not know whether the person selected was a man or a woman, the chance of selecting a person wearing glasses would be about 27%. When finding probabilities, it is crucial to carefully interpret the statements that are made about the desired event. For example, "the chance that a randomly selected person is a woman with glasses" is a different statement from "the chance that a woman selected at random wears glasses."

Planning

Students may work on problem 17 through 20 in small groups. Discuss students' explanations for problem 19.

Comments About the Solutions:

18. This problem illustrates the concept that probabilities change if you know more about who (or what) was selected. You may want to make this issue explicit.

19. The difference between the reasoning of Sandra and Juan is in their interpretation of the way the person was selected. Sandra is interpreting the problem to mean that you know the person is a woman; you just need to find the chance she is not wearing glasses. Juan interprets the problem to mean that he needs to find the chance that a person chosen at random is a "women without glasses." Make sure students discuss this subtle difference.

20. If students understand this problem, they informally understand the notion of dependent and independent events.

B
A Matter of
Information
Notes

Watching TV

The seventh grade class in Robert and Hillary's school surveyed all of the students in grades 7 and 8 to find out how much television they watched each day. Some of their results are in the two-way table.

21 Discuss this as a class after students discuss with partners.

21. a. Finish the table of Robert and Hillary's survey.

	Less Than 3 Hours of TV per Day	3 Hours or More of TV per Day	Total
Grade 7		35	
Grade 8			40
Total	50	50	

b. Is there a difference between the number of hours students in grade 7 and students in grade 8 watch TV?

22 Remind students that "a student" means both grades 7 and 8.

22. a. What is the chance that a student chosen at random from Robert's school watches three hours or more of TV a night?

b. If you knew that the student was in grade 7, would you change your answer for part **a**? Explain why or why not.

c. If you find a student who watches TV more than three hours a night, what is the chance that this student is in grade 8?

Assessment Pyramid

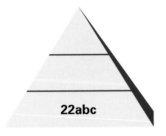

22abc

Use two-way tables to determine probabilities.

Reaching All Learners

Accommodation

Have copies of the chart available for those who need it.

Intervention

If students have difficulty with completing the table because they do not know where to begin, ask them to find out which column they can complete. Make sure students understand the meaning of the totals for each column and row and recognize that the bottom right corner is for the grand total.

You might also want to make a new two-way chart with larger numbers for additional practice.

Solutions and Samples

21. a.

	Less Than 3 Hours of TV per Day	3 Hours or More of TV per Day	Total
Grade 7	25	35	60
Grade 8	25	15	40
Total	50	50	100

b. Answers will vary. Sample answers:

- No, the number of students who watch TV less than 3 hours a day is the same in both grades.
- There are more students in grade 7 who watch 3 hours or more of TV a day, and in grade 8 there are fewer.
- 25 out of 60 (grade 7) is smaller than 25 out of 40 (grade 8), so proportionately fewer 7th graders watch less than 3 hours of TV per day.

22. a. The chance that a student from Robert's school chosen at random watches three hours or more of TV a day is $\frac{50}{100}$, or $\frac{1}{2}$.

b. If you know the student is in grade 7, the answer is different because you look only at the data for students in grade 7 (the first row in the table). The chance that a student in grade 7 watches three hours or more of TV a night is 35 out of 60, or $\frac{35}{60}$, or $\frac{7}{12}$, or about 60%.

c. The chance that a student who watches TV more than three hours a day is in grade 8 is 15 out of 50, or 30%. Use the data in the second column of the table: Fifty students watch TV more than three hours a night; 15 of those are in grade 8.

Hints and Comments

Overview

Students again explore situations with two possibly related events: grade level and number of hours watching TV. They make statements about chance for this problem context.

About the Mathematics

Students again study a situation in which two events are possibly related. In a two-way table, information can be left out; if enough information is available, the rest can be deduced from that.

Planning

Students may work on problems 21 and 22 individually or in pairs. Discuss problem 21b in class. Problem 22 may be used as informal assessment. You may want to do the problems on this page based on data collected by students themselves. (See Extension below.)

Comments About the Solutions

21. b. As with problem 16 on page 16 of the Student Book, some students may want to compare the absolute numbers. The formulation of the problem allows for this. Be sure to discuss students' answers in class and pay attention to the difference between absolute and relative comparison. (It is not necessary to use these words; this is addressed in the unit *Ratios and Rates*.)

Extension

Instead of using the data in the Student Book, you may have students conduct this survey themselves as an activity. The work should be divided among class members.

Survey

Collect data from all students in grades 7 and 8 in your school on the following:

- What grade are you in?

  Grade 7

  Grade 8

- How much TV do you watch?

  Less than 3 hours a night

  3 or more hours a night

Be sure to record your data properly and make a two-way table.

A Matter of Information

Notes

A Matter of Information

Math History

Frequency Analysis

Knowing letter frequencies is useful for winning games like Hangman and also for cracking codes.

In the ninth century, an Arabian scientist named Al-kindi wrote about a method for code-breaking now known as frequency analysis. He discovered that the variation in frequency of letters in a document can be used to decipher encrypted text. This is a translation of some Al-kindi text taken from *The Code Book* by Simon Singh.

> One way to solve an encrypted message, if you know its language, is to find ordinary text of the same language long enough to fill one sheet or so, and then count the occurrences of each letter. You can call the most frequently occurring letter the "first." The next most occurring letter the "second," the following most occurring letter the "third," and so on, until you have used all the different letters in the sample.

Then we look at the coded text we want to solve, and we also classify its symbols. We find the most occurring symbol and change it to the form of the "first" letter of the plain text sample; the next most common symbol is changed to the form of the "second" letter; and the following most common symbol is changed to the form of the "third" letter; and so on, until we account for all symbols of the cryptogram we want to solve.

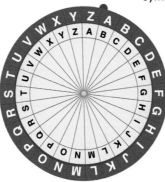

You can use this frequency analysis method of Al-Kindi to decipher the following encrypted English text!

KL, KHUH L KDYH D VKRUW WHAW IRU BRX WR GHFLSKHU, L JXHVV BRX FDQ GHFUBSW LW.

You may make your own encrypted texts using a device like this.

Reaching All Learners

Extension

Challenge students to devise similar or more advanced methods for coding messages.

19 Second Chance

Hints and Comments

Overview

Students read the Math History. There are no problems to solve on this page.

Notes

Read the Summary as a class. Students should already have this information in their notes.

 A Matter of Information

Summary

You can collect information on how often certain outcomes occur. This information can be presented in tables or graphs.

The information can be collected for all of the cases being studied, as in asking everyone in Robert's school how many hours they watched television.

You can use this information to state the chances of certain outcomes for those cases.

Sometimes, not all of the information is available and you have to take a sample as in counting the number of times the letters of the alphabet are used in a newspaper. When this is the case, you can only estimate the chances of an outcome.

When chance is estimated from experiments or surveys, it is sometimes called experimental chance.

If the chance is known before collecting data, like for tossing number cubes or coins, you can call this the theoretical chance.

Figuring the chance that an event occurs depends on what you know.

For example, if you know a person from Robert's school is in 7th grade, you only use the information about the 7th grade to make chance statements and not any of the information about the 8th grade.

You can record results of related outcomes in a two-way table and use the information in the table to make chance statements.

	Men	Women	Total
Glasses	32	3	35
No Glasses	56	39	95
Total	**88**	**42**	130

Reaching All Learners

Vocabulary Building

As a review activity, have students give examples of problems from Sections A and B in which they found theoretical and experimental probabilities.

Hints and Comments

Overview

Students read the Summary, which reviews the main concepts covered in this section.

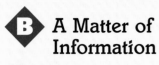

Notes

Ages of Doctors in the United States

Use the information in the table to answer the following questions.

Ages of Doctors in the United States			
Doctors	Female	Male	Total
Under 35 Years Old	60,000	80,000	140,000
35 Years and Over	150,000	550,000	700,000
Total	210,000	630,000	840,000

Source: American Medical Association, December 31, 2001

1. **a.** If you choose a doctor at random, estimate the chance that the doctor will be female.

   b. Was there a difference in the chance that a randomly chosen doctor would be female rather than male ten or twenty years ago? Explain your thinking.

   c. If you randomly choose from a set of doctors you know to be under 35, what is the chance that the doctor will be a male?

   d. If you choose a doctor at random from those you know to be male, what is the chance that the doctor will be older than 35?

   e. What observations can you make about the chance that a doctor will be young or old and be male or female?

Robert's mother has to replace three keys on her computer keyboard because the letters on them had worn off.

2. Reflect Which three letters do you think she had to replace? Explain your answer.

2 Have students check keyboards of computers and/or typewriters in their class or school lab to verify this "frequency of use" phenomena.

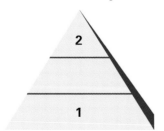
Reaching All Learners

Study Skills

As a review before the first Unit Test, have students update their notes with any additional information from the section Summary. Also ask student to match the Check Your Work problems to similar questions they completed in Sections A and B.

Solutions and Samples

Answers to Check Your Work

1 a. The chance that a randomly chosen doctor is female is $\frac{210,000}{840,000}$, which is about $\frac{2}{8}$ or 25%. You can find the percentage using your calculator or you can estimate.

b. It seems like there is a difference. Sample answer: The chance that a doctor would be female rather than male many years ago was smaller. For the group of doctors over 35 years of age, only 150,000 out of 700,000 are female, which is $\frac{15}{70}$, or about 20%. For the group of doctors under 35 years old, the chance that a doctor is female is 60,000 out of 140,000, or about 40%.

c. The chance that a randomly chosen doctor from a set of doctors you know to be under 35 will be a male is 80,000 out of 140,000, or $\frac{8}{14}$ (use the data in the first row of the table), which is about 60% (57% is also okay). You might also reason from the work in **b** that about 40% were female, so the chance of a male doctor would be 100%–40% or 60%.

d. The chance a doctor chosen at random from the ones that are male will be older than 35 is $\frac{550,000}{630,000}$, or $\frac{55}{63}$, which is about 90% (or 87%).

e. Answers will vary. Sample answers:

- Based on the data in the table, if you chose a doctor at random, the most likely outcome will be a male doctor 35 years old or older. This has a chance of about 66%.

- Based on the data in the table, the chance that a randomly chosen doctor is a female under 35 years old is only about 7%.

- It looks like younger doctors are more balanced – male/female, though a few more are male, but older doctors are mostly male.

2. Different answers are possible. Sample answer: She probably had to replace the E, T, and A, since these are the most commonly used letters in the English language. You can find information on frequently used letters in the table in this section or on the Internet (also for other languages).

Hints and Comments

Overview

Students complete the Check Your Work problems as a self-assessment of key concepts and skills from this section. Students can use Student Book pages 52–54 to check their answers.

Planning

After students complete Section B, you may assign as homework appropriate activities from the Additional Practice section, located on Student Book pages 46 and 47.

Middle school and high school students in the Parker School District were asked whether or not they had seen a recent movie.

	Saw Movie	Did Not See Movie	Total
Middle School	34	...	100
High School	...	...	...
Total	120	...	200

3. a. Copy the table and fill in the missing information.

b. Describe the difference between middle school and high school students with respect to seeing the movie.

c. If you talked to a student who was surveyed about the movie and he told you that he hadn't seen it, what is the chance that this student is in middle school?

Blood Type and Rhesus Factor (RH)	Percentage of Population
O positive	36%
O negative	6%
A positive	38%
A negative	6%
B positive	8%
B negative	2%
AB positive	3.5%
AB negative	0.5%

People have four different blood types: A, B, AB, and O.

For each type, the Rhesus factor (RH), a substance in red blood cells, may be positive or negative. In the table, you see the percentage of the U.S. population with each type of blood.

4. a. If a person is selected randomly, what is the chance that this person's blood is type B?

b. What is the chance that a randomly selected person is RH positive?

c. How would the answer to **b** change if you knew the person has type B blood?

 For Further Reflection

The two-way tables in this section used two sets of information like age and hours watching TV or gender and wearing glasses. Could you make a table if you had three sets of information, like age, gender, and number of hours watching TV? Explain how you could do this or why it is not possible.

For Further Reflection

This reflective question is designed to promote student reflection on the limitations of two-way tables.

Assessment Pyramid

☒ FFR

3, 4

Assesses Section B Goals

Reaching All Learners

Advanced Learners

Assume the U.S. population is 300 million. Challenge students to convert the table for problem 4 into a table with four rows (blood type) and two columns (Rhesus factor) that shows the number of people for each blood type and Rhesus factor.

Solutions and Samples

3 a. The finished table will look like this:

	Saw Movie	Did Not See Movie	Saw Movie
Middle School	34	66 (100 − 34)	100
High School	86 (120 − 34)	14 (80 − 66 or 100 − 86)	100 (200 − 100)
Total	120	80 (200 − 120)	200

The rows and columns all have to add up properly. You can start filling in the middle numbers in the first and last row and the first and last column. Using two of these numbers, you can fill in the number in the middle.

b. Answers will vary. You can write different correct statements. For example:

- Of the middle school students, most (about $\frac{2}{3}$) did not see the movie.
- Of the high school students, most (86%) did see the movie.

c. Of all the students, 80 did not see the movie, so you only look in the second column in the table. The chance that a student who told you he hadn't seen the movie is in middle school is 66 out of 80, which is about 80% (82.5%).

4 a. The chance that the blood type of a randomly selected person is B is 10%. This is 8% for B positive and 2% for B negative. You can only add the percents because the categories do not overlap in any way. If there were 100 people, 8 of them would be B positive and 2 B negative, so 10 of the 100 or 10% would have blood type B.

b. You can reason the same way about the percents. The chance that the Rhesus factor of a randomly selected person is positive is 36% + 38% + 8% + 3.5% = 85.5%.

c. Yes, it would change a little. If you know a randomly selected person has blood type B, you don't look at any of the other blood types. Then the chance that the Rhesus factor is positive is 8 out of 10, which is 80%

Hints and Comments

Overview

Students continue completing the Check Your Work and For Further Reflection problems for Section B.

For Further Reflection

Answers will vary. If you had three sets of information, like age, gender, and number of hours watching TV, you could make a table with split cells. It is harder to find and write the totals.

	Less than 3 Hours	3 Hours or More
Grade 6	15 girls	5 girls
	20 boys	7 boys
Grade 7	8 girls	13 girls
	12 boys	11 boys

Another way would be to use a third dimension, but this is very difficult to draw.

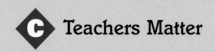

Section Focus

Students investigate what happens to the chances (relative frequencies) on the outcomes as the number of trials increases. They note that the variation in the results becomes smaller, the results become more stable, and the experimental chance approaches the theoretical chance. Students use experiments and simulations and calculate experimental chances in several situations.

Pacing and Planning

Day 10: Heads in the Long Run		Student pages 23–25
INTRODUCTION	Problem 1	Toss a coin and investigate how often heads occurs for an increasing number of tosses.
CLASSWORK	Problems 2 and 3	Make a graph of cumulative relative frequencies and reason about what will happen in the long run.
HOMEWORK	Problems 4* and 5	Determine the fairness of various games of chance and correct unfair games by adjusting the points awarded.

Day 11: The Toothpick Game		Student page 26
INTRODUCTION	Review homework.	Review homework from Day 10.
ACTIVITY	Activity, page 26	Play the toothpick chance game.
HOMEWORK	Problem 6	Devise a scoring system to make a game fair.

Day 12: Guessing on the Test		Student pages 27–29
INTRODUCTION	Review homework. Problems 7 and 8	Review homework from Day 11 and reason about the chance of correctly guessing answers on a true-false test.
ACTIVITY	Activity, page 28	Simulate guessing answers on a true-false test and estimate the chance of passing a test by guessing.
CLASSWORK	Problems 9 and 10	Compare results displayed on a bar graph for a computer simulation with class results.
HOMEWORK	Problems 11 and 12	Reason about the probability of passing a true-false test if the number of questions increases.

Day 13: The Game of Hog		Student pages 30–34
ACTIVITY	Activity, page 30	Play the game of Hog and try to find a strategy for accumulating the highest total score.
CLASSWORK	Problems 13 and 14	Make conjectures about the best strategy for the Game of Hog.
HOMEWORK	Check Your Work	Student self-assessment: Reason about fairness and probability.

Day 14: Summary		Student page 34
INTRODUCTION	Review homework.	Review homework from Day 13.
ASSESSMENT	Quiz 2	Assessment of Section A through C Goals
HOMEWORK	For Further Reflection	Describe situations in which outcomes need to be analyzed using experimental and theoretical probabilities.

* Discuss the introduction to Problem 4 in class before assigning homework.

Additional Resources: Additional Practice, Section C, Student Book pages 48 and 49

Materials

Student Resources
Quantities listed are per student, unless otherwise noted.

- **Student Activity Sheet 4**
- **Student Activity Sheet 5** (per pair of students)

Teachers' Resources
No resources required

Student Materials
Quantities listed are per student, unless otherwise noted.

- Coin or two-colored disk
- Number cubes (two per pair of students)
- Thumbtack
- Toothpicks (one per pair of students)
- Rulers
- Large sheet of paper (one per pair of students)

*See Hints and Comments for optional materials.

Learning Lines

Games of Chance

Chance games often involve situations with combined events. Before playing such games, it is useful to determine each player's chance for winning to determine whether the game is fair or unfair. A game's fairness depends on each player's chance of winning and on the scoring system.

At the End of the Section: Learning Outcomes

Students recognize that in the long run experimental probabilities approach theoretical probabilities. They are able to find the theoretical chance for a situation or estimate the experimental chance. They make informed decisions about whether games are fair and investigate whether certain strategies offer a better chance of winning a game. Students know how to set up and conduct a simulation if theoretical chances are difficult to calculate.

C

In the Long Run

Heads in the Long Run

You can reason about the chance of some events, like tossing a die, by knowing about the possible outcomes. Sometimes you can collect information from a survey and estimate the chances. Another way to think about chance is to try the situation over and over and use the results to estimate the chance that certain outcomes will occur.

Suppose you toss a coin lots and lots of times. What will happen to the chances of getting heads? The table shows the results of tossing a coin in sets of 25s.

Total Number of Tosses	Number of Heads in This Set of 25 Tosses	Total Number of Heads So Far	Chance of Getting Heads
25	16	16	$\frac{16}{25} = .64$
50	12	28	$\frac{28}{50} = .56$
75	11	39	
100	8	47	
125	13	60	
150	14	74	
175	13	87	
200	12	99	
225	12	111	
....	....	....	

1. **a.** Toss a coin 25 times and add your count to the table. Copy the table into your notebook.

   b. Toss the coin another 25 times and add the count to the table.

   The estimated chance of getting heads is the total number of heads over the total number of tosses.

   c. In the table, fill in the column **Chance of Getting Heads**.

1a Suggest to students to write "Running Total" above the column labeled "Total Number of Heads So Far." Students will need a calculator for this problem. You may want to have students add "%" to the final column.

You may want to point out that in the third column, "The Total Number of Heads So Far" can be found by adding the new number of heads from column two to the last number in column 3.

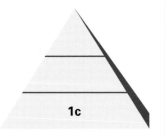
Reaching All Learners

Accommodation

Some students may need to have a copy of the chart available to write on rather than copying the table from the book.

Solutions and Samples

1. a., b., and **c.**
Answers will vary. Actual data from a classroom trial is given below.

Total Number of Tosses	Number of Heads in this Set of 25 Tosses	Total Number of Heads So Far	Chance of Getting Heads
25	16	16	$\frac{16}{25} = .48$
50	12	28	$\frac{28}{50} = .56$
75	11	39	$\frac{39}{75} = .52$
100	8	47	$\frac{47}{100} = .47$
125	13	60	$\frac{60}{125} = .48$
150	14	74	$\frac{74}{150} = .49$
175	13	87	$\frac{87}{175} = .50$
200	12	99	$\frac{99}{200} = .495$
225	12	111	$\frac{111}{225} = .49$
250	11	122	$\frac{122}{250} = .49$
275	16	138	$\frac{138}{275} = .50$

Hints and Comments

Materials

coin or two-colored disk (one per student)

(Note: All students should use the same type of coin or disk.)

Overview

Students toss a coin and investigate how often heads occurs. They calculate the relative frequency or the chance of heads for a growing number of tosses.

About the Mathematics

For tossing a coin, the theoretical chance of tossing heads is 0.5 for each toss if the coin is fair (symmetric) and if the method of tossing is fair (similar each time). When tossing a coin, the probability of the coin landing on heads can have great variability in the short term, but as the number of trials increases, the relative frequency of heads converges towards the theoretical probability of 0.5. Students have informally observed this convergence in the previous Probability unit, *Take a Chance*. The convergence can be documented by calculating the relative frequency in a cumulative frequency table. A graph is also helpful for demonstrating this convergence toward theoretical probabilities.

Planning

Students can work on problem 1 individually or in pairs. Students need the result of problem 1 for problem 2 on the next page.

Comments About the Solutions

1. Students make two more entries for the table. Instead of having each student do this individually, it is possible to do this as a class activity and have all students enter the same two entries.

1. c. Students may want to use a calculator to find the chances (cumulative relative frequencies) in the last column.

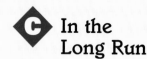

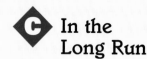 In the Long Run

Notes

2b Rephrase to "Make two conclusions about the graph."

2d You may want to discuss that only in the long run will the result from the experiment approach the theoretical chance of 0.5. This will happen only if the experiment is done in a fair way, for example, if each toss is made under the same conditions.

3 This is important to discuss as a class. Encourage different answers at this stage, but discuss them in class.

2. a. Graph the number of tosses and the chance you will get a head on **Student Activity Sheet 4**.

b. Describe what you see in the graph.

c. **Reflect** Theoretically, the chances of getting a head or tail are equal. Why does the percentage of heads vary?

d. Describe what you think will happen to the graph and the chance of getting a head if the coin is tossed 300 times more.

Deborah tosses a coin. After tossing it nine times in a row, she got this result.

H T T H H T T T T

For the tenth toss, Deborah thinks she has a much bigger chance of getting a head than a tail. Ilana says, "This is not true since the coin does not remember that it already came up tails lots of times."

3. a. Do you agree with Deborah that the chance that she will get a head on the tenth toss is bigger than the chance that she will get a tail? Why or why not?

b. What does Ilana mean when she says that the coin does not remember?

Assessment Pyramid

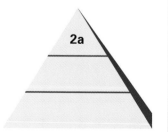

Understand that variability is inherent in any probability situation.

Reaching All Learners

Vocabulary Building

Review the terms *theoretical* (what should happen "in a perfect world") and *experimental* (what does happen).

Intervention

Model Deborah's situation with ten coins to illustrate the situation being described.

Solutions and Samples

2. a. Sample graph using the data from problem 1a:

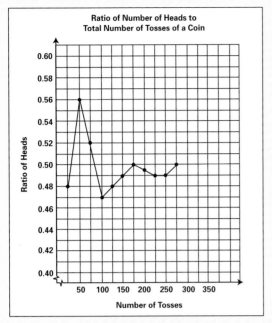

Ratio of Number of Heads to Total Number of Tosses of a Coin

(y-axis: Ratio of Heads, ranging from 0.40 to 0.60; x-axis: Number of Tosses, 50 to 350)

b. Descriptions will vary. Sample student answers:
   - It first goes up, then down, and then it stays close to 0.50.
   - Most of the points are near 0.50.
   - The graph goes up and down more in the beginning than it does later.

c. The variance is due to the variability of outcomes. You can expect a certain percentage of outcomes for heads and tails, but you cannot predict what the outcomes will be when you flip the coin.

Sample student answers:
   - It can vary, but the more times you flip the coin, the closer you get to 0.50.
   - Because you never know what you are going to get for each flip.

d. The overall outcome for flipping heads will approach 0.50.

3. a. Answers will vary. Sample answers:
   - The chance Deborah will get heads on the tenth toss is not bigger than the chance she will get tails because the chance to flip heads or tails is always $\frac{1}{2}$. (CORRECT)
   - The chance Deborah will get heads on the tenth toss is actually bigger than the chance she will get tails because she had fewer heads than tails so far. (INCORRECT: Ilana is correct, the coin does not "remember" the previous flip.)
   - The chance Deborah will flip heads on the tenth toss is smaller than the chance she will get tails because apparently she tosses fewer heads. Perhaps the coin is not fair. (MAY BE CORRECT)

Hints and Comments

Materials

Student Activity Sheet 4 (one per student)

Overview

Students continue their investigation of the chance for heads in the long run. They make a graph of the cumulative relative frequencies. They describe the pattern and reason about what will happen in the long run. Students reflect on a situation in which tails seems to be flipped more often. Using this information, they reason about what will happen on the next toss.

About the Mathematics

The graph of cumulative relative frequencies for the number of heads as the number of tosses increases stabilizes if the number of trials is large enough. In the long run, the relative frequency of heads is not influenced very much by the outcome of one extra toss. It may take many trials to see a stable pattern emerge and for the experimental chance to converge to 0.5. If, in a small number of trials, one outcome seems to occur more then expected (for example, 6 out of 9 heads), some people believe that the next outcomes will likely "correct" the earlier ones. So they believe that the chance of tossing tails will be larger. But if the experiment is fair, if the conditions are identical for each trials, and if the trials are independent, the chances are equal each time and the next trial is not influenced by previous ones. The coin has "no memory of previous events."

Planning

Students may work on problems 2 and 3 in small groups. Discuss their answers in class.

Comments About the Solutions

3. a. Although the second answer noted in the Solutions column is incorrect, many students may believe this to be true. The third one may be true, but the number of tosses is too small to tell if the coin is not fair.

b. Ilana means that on each toss there is an equal chance of heads and tails. The coin does not "remember" what was previously tossed.

Fair Games?

You may have played games like Monopoly® or other games that use number cubes to tell you how to proceed. Sometimes you are lucky when you play, but your success really depends on chance. A good game of chance needs to be fair; all players should have an equal chance of winning.

4 Students understand the fairness of these games if they actually play them and determine the experimental chance of winning.

4. Are the following games fair? Give reasons to support your answers. You can play the games to find out!

   a. Two people each flip a coin. If both coins land on the same side, A wins one point; otherwise B wins one point.

   b. Two people each roll a number cube at the same time. If neither of the players roll a 5 or a 6, A wins one point; otherwise B gets one point.

   c. Two players each throw two number cubes 24 times. If no double 6 occurs, A wins one point; if a double 6 occurs, B wins one point.

   d. Two players take turns tossing a thumbtack. If the thumbtack lands on its back (point up), A wins; if it lands on its side, B wins.

   It is not always easy to decide whether a game is fair. Sometimes you can just reason about the situation and decide whether it is fair. Sometimes you can calculate the chances, but more often you will need to play the game many times to estimate the chance of winning.

   5. a. For which of the games from problem 4 could you decide whether the game was fair by reasoning or calculating? Which ones did you need to play?

      b. **Reflect** Find a way to adjust the scoring so that the "unfair" games in problem 1 are fair. Explain why your scoring system will make the game fair.

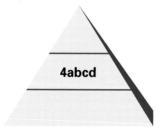
Reaching All Learners

Extension

Have students find the actual probabilities for problems 4a, b, and c.

Intervention

If students are having difficulties with **5b**, have them try this simpler game first: Roll one number cube. If it is a 5 or 6, I get one point. If it is anything else, you get a point. *Is this a fair game?* (No.) *How would you adjust the points for this game to make it fair?* (The game could be made fair by awarding player A the point if double five or double 6 is rolled.)

Solutions and Samples

4. a. Yes, this game is fair. There are 4 options:

- A-heads, B-heads;
- A-heads, B-tails;
- A-tails, B-heads; and
- A-tails, B-tails

All options are equally likely. In half of the cases, A wins. In the other half of the cases, B wins. You can either reason about the chances for each combination using, for example, a tree diagram, or you can test the fairness of the game with many trials.

b. This game is not fair (but it is almost fair). Use the table on page 6 of the Student Book to find the outcomes for rolling two number cubes with no 5s or 6s. There are 16 number cube combinations with no 5s or 6s, and 20 combinations with either a 5, a 6, or both 5 and 6. So player B has a bigger chance of winning: the chance of B scoring a point is $\frac{20}{36}$ and the chance of A scoring a point is $\frac{16}{36}$.

c. This game is quite unfair and favors player A. The chance of Player A scoring a point each round is $\frac{35}{36}$. The chance of B scoring a point each round is $\frac{1}{36}$.

d. Students may need to play this game to see which is more likely: a thumbtack landing on its back or on its side. A thumbtack landing on its side seems to be the most likely outcome. So this is not a fair game.

5. a. For games **a**, **b**, and **c**, the chances could be calculated using a table or a tree diagram. For game **d**, the experimental probability of both outcomes needs to be estimated by playing the game.

b. Game **b** can be made fair by changing the scores. You need to give A more points for succeeding. If you play the game often, A should be expected to win $\frac{16}{36}$ = 44% of the trials, and B should win $\frac{20}{36}$ = 55% of the trials. The ratio of A winning is 16 to 20, so if you give A 5 points and B 4, the game would be fair.

For games **c** and **d**, if students can estimate the chance of each outcome, the scores could also be adjusted using the ratios of the chances to make the game "fair." For game **c**, students may also suggest modifying the rules. For example, points could be awarded for both cubes showing even numbers and both cubes showing odd numbers.

Hints and Comments

Materials

coins (one per pair of student);
number cubes (two per pair of student;
thumbtacks (one per pair of students)

Overview

Students reason about the fairness of games. Students think of a way to make unfair games fair by adjusting the scores.

About the Mathematics

A significant portion of probability theory was developed in the 17th century in the context of finding chances for game situations. Even if games are played with coins or number cubes that are fair objects and they are used in a fair way, the game itself may not be fair due to the rules. *Unfair* means that not every player has the same chance of winning. Students investigate the fairness of games. In fairly simple situations, they can reason about the theoretical chances for the favorable outcomes for each player. They may use tree diagrams or a table to do so. In complex situations, students may need to play the game to find the experimental (empirical) chances for the outcomes that are favorable for each player. If games are unfair, they may be made fair by adjusting the scoring to compensate for the chance of favorable outcomes for each player.

Planning

Students may work in small groups on problems 4 and 5.

Technology

Several software programs or applets can be found on the Internet to simulate rolling number cubes or tossing coins. These simulations can be used to estimate the experimental chances for the games.

Also information can be found from the Internet on the games that were studied by Fermat and Pascal (around 1650) and from which the probability theory was developed.

Comments About the Solutions

4. If necessary, have students play the games. Note that in order to have the experimental probability approach the theoretical one, students would have to play the game a lot of times. Groups of students can each investigate one of the games.

5. Games can be made fair by adjusting the scores or by changing the rules. This is a difficult problem; you may want to adjust the scores only for game **b**.

C In the Long Run

Notes

Have students play the game and complete problem 6 in pairs.

6a Fifty trials is not enough to show how the experimental chance of landing on a line approaches the theoretical chance, which is $\frac{2}{\pi}$. You may want to combine the results for the whole class to get a better estimate. It is also possible to look for a simulation of this game; several can be found in the Internet.

6b Tally the class results on a poster displayed in the classroom. The combined data makes it easier to determine the answer to this problem.

The Toothpick Game

With a partner, you are going to investigate whether the Toothpick Game is fair. First you need a board for the game.

Activity

For this activity, you need:

- a toothpick,
- a ruler,
- a large sheet of paper.

Measure the length of the toothpick. Use a ruler to draw parallel lines on the sheet of paper. The distance between each two lines must be the same as the length of the toothpick. This will be your game board. (See example in **Student Activity Sheet 5**.)

Play the game with a partner. One student drops the toothpick on the game board. The other records whether the toothpick lands on a line or between two lines.

Rules:

- Decide who will be player A and who will be B.
- Put the game board on the floor. From about 18 inches above the board, drop the toothpick on the game board.
- If the toothpick lands on a line, player A gets a point.
- If the toothpick lands between two lines, player B gets a point. If the toothpick does not land on the board, take another turn.
- Take turns. Do this 50 times and record the results. The player with the most points is the winner.

6. **a.** Do you think the Toothpick Game is a fair game? Give reasons to support your answer.

   b. If it is not a fair game, change the number of points for landing on a line and for landing between lines so the game becomes fair.

Assessment Pyramid

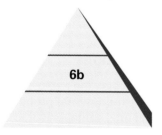

Make decisions using probability and expected values.

Reaching All Learners

Accommodation

Some students may need step-by-step guidance in measuring and making the game board for the toothpick game.

Solutions and Samples

6. a. The game is not fair, but answers may vary depending on students' results. The theoretical chance for a toothpick landing on a line is $\frac{2}{\pi} = 0.6$. It is unlikely students will be able to estimate this chance from only 50 tries.

b. Students answers should be based on the results they recorded. So answers will vary, depending on the answers to part **a**. For example, assume one group of students had the following results for 50 drops: the toothpick landed on the line 32 times, the toothpick landed between the lines 18 times. Using the rules outlined for this Activity, player A would receive 32 points and player B would receive 18 points.

Assuming this result holds for future games (which is, of course, unlikely), to make this game fair, the awarded points need to be adjusted so that by the end of the game (50 drops), each player would receive the same number of points. Students can reason through this in the following way: let a drop on the line receive one point, but a drop between the lines receive two points. Using the results from the last game, player A would still receive 32 points, but player B would receive 36 points. So this would be a fairer game. However, some students might point out that this is not exactly fair.

One method for adjusting the score would be to use the ratios of the chances for each player. You may want to discuss with students how to make the game fair based on the theoretical chances. In theory, player A would win in about 6 out of 10 trials, and B would win in about 4 out of 10. To make the game fair, you give player A 2 points each time the toothpick lands on a line and B 3 points if it lands between lines.

Another method for assigning points to this game to make it exactly fair (based on an experimental result) would be to find the respective factors needed to compute a least common multiple from the experimental results. To help students relate the points awarded to the common multiples of 32 and 18, the following table could be created: This table shows options that are very close: marked in green (Player A receives 4 points, player B receives 7 points); and marked in red (Player A receives 5 points, Player B receives 9 points).

Based on these results, one option is exactly fair: Player A should receive 9 points for a toothpick that lands on a line, and player B should receive 16 points for a toothpick that lands between the lines.

Hints and Comments

Materials

toothpicks;
rulers;
large sheets of paper;
Student Activity Sheet 5 (one of each for each pair of students)

Overview

Students play the Toothpick Game and determine a scoring system that will make the game fair.

About the Mathematics

This problem is known as Buffon's Needle Problem. Compte de Buffon (1707–1788) was a French scientist interested in many things including mathematics and botany. The game or experiment is a way to estimate and approximate the value of pi. This is a game in which students cannot find the theoretical chance; however, the chance of landing on or between the lines can be found experimentally. If students play the game a number of times, they can estimate the chances (relative frequencies) of both outcomes. The theoretical chance for landing on a line is 2 divided by π, which is about 0.6.

Points	Player A	Player B
1	32	18
2	64	36
3	96	54
4	128	72
5	160	90
6	192	108
7	224	126
8	256	144
9	288	162
10	320	180
11	352	198
12	384	216
13	416	234
14	448	252
15	480	270
16	512	288

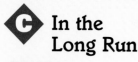
Notes

Guessing on a Test

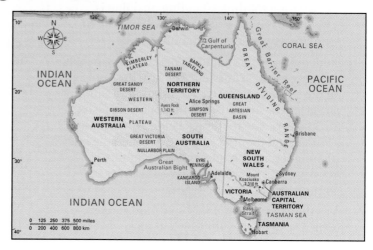

Charlie has a geography test. The test consists of ten statements that are either true or false.

For example, one of the questions was:

Sydney is the capital of Australia.

☑ **True**   ☐ **False**

7 Discuss answers in class. Students do not need to be able to calculate the actual chances, but they should be able to reason about them. Students often guess too high on this question, but this will be revisited on the next page.

Charlie has not prepared for the test, so he guesses the answers to all of the questions. He will pass the test if he gets at least seven answers correct. Charlie thinks that the chance that he will pass the test by just guessing at all the answers is more than 50%.

7. Do you agree with Charlie? If you do, explain why. If you don't, how big do you think the chance is that Charlie will pass the test when he guesses all 10 answers?

Josh says to Charlie, "We could model guessing the answers to the geography test by flipping a coin and use that to find the chance that you will pass if you guess."

8a Ask students why flipping a coin is a model-for guessing on a true-false test.

8. a. What does Josh mean?

   b. Could Josh and Charlie use a number cube to model "guessing the answers"? Explain.

Reaching All Learners

Vocabulary Building

Have students explain what it means to "model guessing the answers."
A *model* is a simulation of a situation.

Solutions and Samples

7. Charlie is incorrect. Sample student responses:

I do not agree with Charlie. For each problem, he has a chance of 50% to guess correctly. However, to guess two or more questions correctly the chance gets smaller and smaller. A tree diagram can show this.

(Sample incorrect answer): I agree with Charlie that the chance he will pass the test by guessing is more then 50%. For each problem, he has a chance of 50% to guess correctly, and so for ten problems the chance is bigger.

8. a. Answers will vary. Sample answer:

Josh means that they can flip a coin for each question and count the outcome as a guess. For instance, if the outcome is heads, this means the answer is correct. If the outcome is tails, the answer is incorrect. The coin flip can be used because the chance for guessing between two answers and flipping a coin are the same.

b. Yes, Josh and Charlie can use a number cube to model "guessing the answers." They need to assign half of the possible outcomes to a correct guess and the other half to an incorrect guess. For instance, a roll of 1, 2, or 3 could represent a correct guess, and a roll of 4, 5, or 6 could represent an incorrect guess. Or Josh and Charlie could choose to use even rolls as correct and odd rolls as incorrect.

Hints and Comments

Overview

Students reason about the chance of answering correctly by guessing answers on a true-false test. They think about ways to simulate this to find the chances.

About the Mathematics

In multi-event situations, if you cannot compute the chances of a long sequence of events, you may simulate the situation to estimate the chances experimentally. To be able to design a simulation, the chances for the outcomes of the single event must be known. A simulation can differ from an experiment: in the case of an experiment, the actual situation is repeated a number of times, while in the case of a simulation, a model may be used. In the situation on this page and the next page, students simulate correctly guessing the questions to a true-false test by tossing a coin.

Planning

Students may work on problems 7 and 8 individually or in pairs. Discuss students' answers for problem 7.

Comments About the Solutions

7. This situation is further explored in problems 9 through 12 on the next pages where a simulation is used to estimate the chances. It is revisited in Section D where students learn how to calculate the theoretical chances.

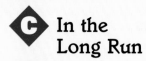

C In the Long Run

Notes

Activity Make sure students understand that 10 tosses represents one test. Have students record the 10 tosses each time, not just the final count of correct answers.

9a Students should answer this question for each of the simulated tests. Some students may just add up all the heads. As long as they have both answers, this is not a problem.

9b It may be necessary to discuss the meaning of this table in class first. Display each class's data in the classroom so students will be able to see trends.

Activity

You can toss a coin to model or simulate getting a question correct by guessing.

> Heads means your answer is correct.
>
> Tails means your answer is wrong.

Toss a coin 10 times, once for each question on the geography test, and record the results. This is like taking one test.

Flip the coin another 10 times and record the results. Do this until you have modeled taking five tests.

9. **a.** In the activity, how many answers did you "guess" correctly (that is, how many times did you throw a "head") on each of your five tests?

   b. Record in a table the class results for everyone's five tests.

Number of Questions Correct	Number of Tests with This Result
0	
1	
2	
3	
4	
5	
6	
7	
8	
9	
10	

   c. Use the results in the table to estimate the chance that someone passes the test with 7 or more questions out of 10 correct by just guessing.

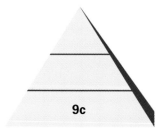
Reaching All Learners

Parent Involvement

Parents might be interested in completing this simulation with their child at home and discussing the results. Students and parents could also set up a simulation for the activity using a number cube. (1–3 = correct answer, 4–6 = incorrect answer.)

Solutions and Samples

9. a. Results will vary. Sample student results:

wwwrwrrwwr	4 out of 10 right
wwwwwrwrww	2 out of 10 right
wrrwwrwrrw	5 out of 10 right
wrrwrwrrww	5 out of 10 right
wrrwwrwrrw	5 out of 10 right

Some students may add up the results as well. In this example, this would give the result: 21 out of 50 were correct.

b Answers will vary depending on the results from the activity.

Sample class result.

Number of Questions Correct	Number of Tests with This Result
0	0
1	1
2	2
3	9
4	27
5	32
6	12
7	6
8	6
9	0
10	0

c. Answers will vary depending on the class results for this activity. Sample answer based on the results shown for problem 9b:

Six students had 7 questions correct, and six students had 8 questions correct. So 12 out of 95 times students were able to pass the test. The estimated chance of passing based on the simulation results is $\frac{12}{95}$, which is 0.1263, or about 12.6%.

Hints and Comments

Materials

coins (one per student);
overhead transparency of the table on Student Book page 28, optional.

Overview

Students toss coins to model the situation of guessing answers on a true-false test and record the results. They estimate the chance of passing the test by guessing answers.

About the Mathematics

Tossing a coin can be used to model or simulate situations with two outcomes that are equally likely. A multi-event situation with two outcomes can be modeled by repeatedly tossing a coin and recording the results. If the number of trials is large enough, the relative frequencies of the outcomes should approach the theoretical probabilities. Students use the simulation to estimate the chance of passing a test by guessing. The rule for passing is: at least 7 out of 10 true-false questions must be answered correctly. A table is made of the frequencies of the number of questions correct per test (which consists of 10 tosses). This table shows a symmetric distribution of the outcomes with the "peak" in the middle (approaching a bell shape). It is possible to calculate the theoretical chance (by using the binomial chance distribution), but the tools students have to do so (for example, using a tree diagram) involve a lot of work. In order to have a more reliable estimate, a computer program or a graphing calculator may be used to generate a larger number of trials.

Planning

Students may work on the activity and problem 9a in pairs. One student tosses while the other records the results. Both students should toss five series of ten tosses so that the class sample is large enough. Complete problem 9b as a whole class activity.

Comments About the Solutions

9. b. This table can be completed in several ways as a whole class. One approach is to ask each student to share his or her results (number of questions correct) for each of the five simulated tests and tally these in the table on the board or on an overhead transparency. Or you can have students record their results on the board or transparency as they complete their tests. Discuss the pattern that emerges on the table with the whole class.

C In the Long Run

Notes

10b Stress this question: *What other pairs have the same chance (theoretically)?* You can also discuss why the graph is symmetric.

12a Students do not need to calculate this answer. They just need to reason that the chance is smaller.

12b Another way to reason would be to think about the chance of getting all answers correct with two questions (1 out of 4), three questions (1 out of 8), four questions (1 out of 16), and so on. Students should see the pattern that the chances are decreasing.

A graphing calculator was used to simulate guessing the answers. The calculator simulated taking the test 500 times.

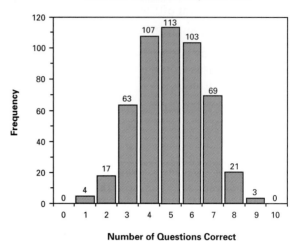

500 Simulations of Guessing on a Ten-Question True/False Test

10. **a.** Use the graph to estimate the chance of passing the test (seven or more correct out of 10).

   b. **Reflect** Explain why the chance of having two questions on the test correct is about the same as the chance of having eight questions correct.

11. Compare the results of the **simulation** on the calculator to the results of the simulation in class. What do you notice?

Suppose the teacher increases the number of true-false questions on the geography test from 10 to 20. You pass the test if you answer at least 14 of the 20 questions correctly.

12. **a.** Do you think the chance of passing the test with 20 questions by guessing is bigger than, smaller than, or the same as passing the test with 10 problems by guessing? Describe your thinking.

   b. What do you think happens to the chance of getting all the questions on the test correct by guessing if the number of questions increases from 10 to 20?

Assessment Pyramid

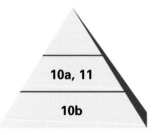

10a, 11

10b

Use simulation and modeling to investigate probability.

Use complementary probability to determine the chance for an event.

Reaching All Learners

Intervention

With problem 11, if students have problems comparing results in a table to those in a graph, you may want to make a graph of the results in the table of problem 9.

For problem 12b, it may help students to think of a tree diagram. It is important that students realize there is only one option (one route) for having all questions correct. The more questions there are, the larger the number of possible outcomes. However, regardless of the number of questions, there is still only one favorable outcome for all questions correct. So the chance of having all questions correct is 1 divided by an increasingly larger number, as more questions are added.

Solutions and Samples

10 a. From the graph, the chance of having seven questions correct is around $\frac{69}{500}$ (this is about 14%). The chance of having eight questions correct is $\frac{21}{500}$ (about 4%). The chance of having nine questions correct is $\frac{3}{500}$ (less than 0.5%), and the chance of having ten questions correct is $\frac{0}{500}$. So the chance of passing the test based on the simulation results is $\frac{93}{500}$, or about 19%.

b. These chances are the same. The chance of having eight questions correct is the same as the chance of having eight questions incorrect.

11. Answers will vary, depending on the results of the activity. Students may note that the overall shape of the graph is about the same. They may also write observations about individual results and chances. Sample student answers:

- The calculator and class results are pretty close: 5 occurs the most, and 4 occurs the second most. Zero and 10 correct guesses never occurred.

- They are both a bell-shaped curve.

- In both graphs, the middle numbers show up the most.

12. a. The chance of passing the test with 20 questions is smaller. Explanations may vary. Sample student explanations:

- The chance is smaller because there are more outcomes.

- There are more questions to get wrong.

- There is a bigger space between passing and getting a perfect score.

- You have the same chance of passing both because the correct and incorrect chances are the same for each problem. (Incorrect)

- It should be the same chance because you are just doubling (Incorrect).

b. The chance of correctly guessing all the questions on a 20-question test is smaller than the chance of correctly guessing all the questions on a 10-question test. For each additional question, the number of possible outcomes grows (think of the chance tree). There is only one favorable outcome for answering all questions correctly, so the chance for this outcome gets smaller as the number of possible outcomes grows larger.

Hints and Comments

Overview

Students continue studying the situation of guessing questions on a test. They study a bar graph of a simulation for 500 trials, and they compare the results to the class simulation. They reason about the probability of passing the true-false test if the number of questions (and the threshold for passing) increases.

About the Mathematics

If the number of trials increases, the distribution of the outcomes approaches the normal distribution, which is a bell-shaped curve. A bar graph of the results will show this shape as well. Instead of the absolute frequencies, the relative frequencies (chances) can also be graphed to create a chance distribution graph. The context can be used as a referent to explain why the shape is symmetrical.

If the situation changes from having at least 7 out of 10 correct to having at least 14 out of 20 correct, the probability of this occurring by guessing does not remain the same!

Comments About the Solutions

12. a. Students do not need to be able to calculate this chance (it is about 6%). Students should reason about the increasing number of options, which reduces the chance for this outcome.

C In the
Long Run

Notes

Make sure students record
the number of cubes used
on each roll and the
number of points scored on
each roll.

The Game of Hog

 Activity

Playing the Game of Hog

Play the game of Hog 20 times with one of your classmates.
You will need eight number cubes, or you can roll one cube
eight times.

Here are the rules:

- Say how many number cubes you want to roll; you can
  choose from one to eight.

- Roll that many number cubes.

- If none of the numbers you rolled is a 1, your score is the
  sum of the numbers you rolled.

- If a 1 comes up on any of your number cubes, then your
  score is 0!

- Now it is your partner's turn.

- You can change the number of cubes you want to roll for
  each turn.

The object of the game is to get as large a total score as you can.
For each roll, record:

- how many number cubes were used;

- how many points were scored.

Adapted from *Measuring Up*, Mathematical Sciences Education Board,
National Research Council, 1993.

Reaching All Learners

Advanced Learners

This same game could be adapted to include different sided number cubes,
which can be found at most game stores. In addition to the common
6-sided number cube, number cubes exist for the other Platonic solids:

- Tetrahedron: 4 sides
- Octahedron: 8 sides
- Dodecagon: 12 sides
- Icosahedron: 20 sides

Students should be able to reason that if these Platonic number cubes were
available to choose from in the game of Hog, the icosahedron is an
excellent choice, and the tetrahedron is a poor choice.

Solutions and Samples

Sample results of students playing Hog 15 times.

Player 1		Player 2	
Number of Cubes	Score	Number of Cubes	Score
3	11	6	29
6	–	6	27
2	–	6	28
6	29	6	–
6	–	2	4
6	–	4	19
5	20	6	20
8	–	8	–
8	34	8	–
4	10	8	–
8	–	8	–
6	–	8	35
7	21	3	13
5	–	3	13
5	27	3	13

Materials

number cubes (at least one per student)

Overview

Students play the game of Hog and try to find a strategy to get as large a total score as they can.

About the Mathematics

By playing the game of Hog, students explore what happens to chances in situations with a sequence of independent events. As the number of events increases, the chances on certain outcomes change. Students informally explore this while playing the game. In Section D, students will calculate chances for this kind of situations.

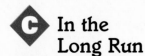
In the Long Run

Notes

13 and 14 Students should discuss these questions with their partner before class discussion. Most students enjoy this game, and struggling students can easily and comfortably participate in this discussion.

13b You may want to check if students take into account both the chance on a score of zero as well as the expected height of the score they can get. You may combine class results to see whether a favorite strategy of one student gave similar scores for other students who rolled this number of cubes.

13. **a. Reflect** How many number cubes would it be unwise to roll when playing Hog? Explain why this is so.

    b. Based on your results playing Hog, what strategy seems to give the biggest chance of winning?

14. **a.** How often did you have 0 points twice in a row? Did this outcome seem to depend on how many number cubes you rolled?

    b. In general, how likely do you think it is to score 0 points at least twice in a row?

Assessment Pyramid

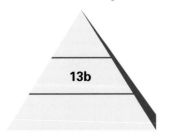

Make decisions using probability and expected values.

Reaching All Learners

Accommodation

Provide a recording sheet for the students for the Hog game including number of cubes rolled and points scored for each student.

Extension

Students can systematically investigate the scores and their chances for each set of number cubes from one to eight. Different groups of students can experiment with different sets of cubes, tossing them at least 50 times, recording the scores, and sharing their findings.

Solutions and Samples

13. a. Answers may vary. Sample response:

- An unwise number of number cubes to roll in the game of Hog would be eight, because when you roll all eight number cubes, the chance of rolling at least one 1 is rather large.

b. Answers will vary, depending on students' results for the game. Sample student answers:

- I usually used six number cubes because the cubes never seemed to land on one.
- A good strategy is to pick a middle number of number cubes, like 4 or 5.
- Fewer than 5 cubes seemed to work best.
- One cube has the best chance of winning at least some points each turn.

14. a. Answers will vary, depending on students' results for the game. Sample responses:

- Player 1 got 0 points twice in a row three different times. Player 2 got a double zero twice. It seemed to happen more often if a large number of number cubes (like 6, 7, or 8) was rolled twice in a row.
- Yes, it did depend on the number of number cubes you rolled. If you rolled eight cubes twice in a row, you had the biggest chance of getting a zero.

b. Answers will vary, depending on students' results for the game. Sample responses:

- Not very likely unless you use a lot of number cubes.
- Maybe 1 out of 15. It's not very likely, but it depends on the number of cubes you choose.

Hints and Comments

Overview

Students reflect on the results of the game of Hog. They make statements about what strategy seems a good one, and how likely it is they score no points twice in a row.

About the Mathematics

The results of playing the game of Hog will probably show that the more the number cubes are rolled, the more zeros are scored. While on the other hand, the scores that are not zero with eight number cubes are higher. Finding a good strategy for the game of Hog by experimenting involves thinking about a trade-off between a high chance of rolling at least one "1" and a high expected score. Students will make this trade-off informally by investigating the results of their game. The chances and expected values can be calculated, but in this section, students are not expected to be able to do this. In the next section, students will calculate some chances for the game of Hog. Expected value is preformally addressed in the unit *Great Predictions*. In the problems on this page, students can reason about how likely future outcomes are based on their results. Note that the number of trials in the activity was rather small, so it may be wise to combine class results or use a computer program or a graphing calculator to generate more trials for the different numbers of number cubes that can be used in the game of Hog.

Planning

Students can work on problem 13 and 14 individually or in pairs. Discuss students' answers in class.

Comments About the Solutions

13. a. The chance of rolling at least one "1" with eight number cubes is rather large. It is about 77% $(1 - \left(\frac{5}{6}\right)^8)$.

b. You may want to check if students take into account both the chance on a score of zero as well as the expected height of the score they can get. You may combine class results to see whether a favorite strategy of one student gave similar scores for other students who rolled this number of cubes. In general, choosing around 5 or 6 number cubes gives a rather stable result.

14. Students will give an answer based on their results, which is the "empirical (or experimental) chance." To score 0 points at least twice in a row means to roll at least one 1 twice in a row. The chance that this will happen depends on the number of number cubes chosen. In the game, students will most likely change the number of cubes if they have a score of zero.

Notes

Summary ✕

If you cannot compute chances of winning beforehand, you can play
a game (like the Toothpick Game or Hog) or simulate the situation
(like guessing on a test) many times to see what happens.

If you do many trials, the chance of an event occuring will be close
to the theoretical chance. With the results from this large number of
trials, you can make statements about chances.

One thing to remember about throwing number cubes and tossing
coins is that number cubes and coins have no memory.

The next throw or toss is not influenced by what has happened before.

Check Your Work ▶

1. Decide whether the following games are fair. You can play the
   games to find out.

   a. Two players take turns rolling a number cube; each player's
   score is the number rolled.

   b. Two players roll two number cubes each at the same time.
   If neither of the players rolls doubles, A gets one point;
   otherwise B gets one.

1b Students might want
to refer back to the two-
cube chart on page 6.

Assessment Pyramid

Assesses Section C Goals

Reaching All Learners

Parent Involvement

As a mid-unit summary exercise, have students explain to parents or family
members different ways to find probabilities. Students can share their
explanations in class the following day, in addition to their responses to the
Check Your Work problems.

Solutions and Samples

Answers to Check Your Work

1. **a.** This game is fair since each player has the same chance of rolling each outcome. Of course, one player can have more luck than the other one, but if the game is played for a long time, both players will end up with the same result.

   b. This game is not fair. A has a bigger chance of winning. You may need to play the game to find this out. You can also reason: there are only 6 ways to get doubles and 30 ways to get "not doubles." You can find the chance for rolling a double with two number cubes from the chart in Section A. So the chance of doubles is less than the chance of "not doubles," which means that A (who wins if no double occurs) has a bigger chance of winning.

Hints and Comments

Overview

Students read the Summary, which reviews the main concepts covered in this section.

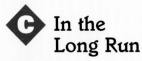

In the Long Run

Notes

4a Remind students that chance is written as a ratio.

2. **a.** If you roll a number cube a thousand times, about how many times do you expect a 6 to come up?

   b. If you roll a number cube 100 times, how often do you expect a number divisible by three? What percentage is that?

3. Melissa and Jody are playing a game. Melissa needs to roll a 6; otherwise she cannot go on. She already rolled the number cube 10 times without rolling a 6.

   Jody thinks that on the next roll Melissa is almost sure to roll a 6.

   a. Do you agree with Jody? Explain your reasoning.

   b. Melissa thinks the number cube is not "fair." Do you agree with Melissa? Explain.

4. Peter takes a geography quiz with five multiple-choice questions. Each question has three options. Here is one of the questions.

   a. If Peter guesses the answer, what is his chance of guessing it wrong?

   b. How can you model guessing the answer to all five questions on the test by using a number cube?

Assessment Pyramid

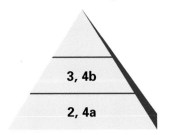

3, 4b

2, 4a

Assesses Section C Goals

Reaching All Learners

Accommodation

Keep number cubes handy for students who need to model these situations.

Solutions and Samples

2. a. If you roll a number cube a thousand times, you would expect a 6 to come up in about $\frac{1}{6}$ of the rolls, so about $\frac{1000}{6} = 167$ times.

b. The numbers divisible by three on a number cube are 3 and 6, which is one third of the numbers on the number cube. If you roll a number cube 100 times, you expect a number divisible by three to come up in about $\frac{1}{3}$ of the rolls. This is about 33%, or about 33 times out of 100. However, since 100 is not a very large number of rolls, your result may be different from 33 due to variability.

3. a. Answers can vary. Here are some correct and incorrect answers.

- "No, I do not agree with Jody because on each roll the chance of rolling a 6 stays the same; it is $\frac{1}{6}$. The number cube has no memory." (correct)

- "Yes, I agree with Jody because if you roll a lot of times, there need to be 6s." (Over many, many times, you will have 6s, but 10 is not a lot of times.)

- "No, I don't agree with Jody. She might not have gotten some of the other numbers either, and they would be just as likely to show up as a 6. (Not quite right because all of the numbers, including 6, are equally likely to show up.)

b. Difference answers are possible. You can not decide this on only 10 rolls. Try it yourself 10 times and see how many rolls it takes to get a 6.

4. a. If Peter guesses the answer to this question, his chance of guessing it wrong is 2 out of 3, or $\frac{2}{3}$. Only one of the options is the correct answer, so the other two are wrong.

b. You can model guessing the answer to all five questions on the test by using a number cube as follows: Let two of the numbers (for example, 1 and 2) of the number cube mean that you guessed a question correctly: the other four numbers (3, 4, 5, and 6) mean that you guessed incorrectly. Now you roll the cube five times, once for each question, and you record whether you "guessed" correctly or incorrectly.

Hints and Comments

Overview

Students complete the Check Your Work problems as a self-assessment of key concepts and skills from this section. Students can check their answers on Student Book pages 54 and 55.

Planning

After students complete Section C, you may assign as homework appropriate activities from the Additional Practice section. These problems are located on Student Book pages 48 and 49.

C In the Long Run

Guessing answers on this quiz was simulated 50 times. These are the results:

Number of Questions out of Five Correct	Number of Times This Occurred
0	9
1	16
2	13
3	5
4	7
5	0

c. Based on these results, what is the chance that Peter will get three or more questions on the quiz correct by guessing?

For Further Reflection

Think of a situation different from the ones in this section where you would have to simulate the situation many times to estimate the chance of an outcome. Think of another situation where you could figure out the theoretical chance and would not need to simulate the situation.

For Further Reflection

This reflection question supports student generalization of types of situations, as they relate to probability.

Assessment Pyramid

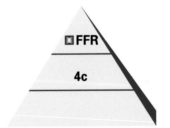

Assesses Section C Goals

Reaching All Learners

Intervention

If some students have difficulty answering problem 4c, suggest that they find the probability for each outcome of this simulation.

Solutions and Samples

4. c. The chance that Peter has 3 or more questions on the quiz correct by guessing is $\frac{12}{50}$, which is 24%.

For Further Reflection

Answers will vary. Sample answers:

Examples of a situation where you need to simulate:

- a game where you roll objects that are not "symmetrical" but have irregular shapes, like the thumbtacks or the paper cups.

- a situation where you cannot calculate the chance because it is too complicated.

An example where you can calculate the theoretical chance:

- a game in which a coin and a number cube are rolled together, and player A wins only if a combination of odds and heads is rolled; otherwise player B wins.

Hints and Comments

Overview

Students continue completing the Check Your Work and For Further Reflection problems for Section C.

Section Focus

Students revisit some of the situations from Section C. They learn how to compute the theoretical chances for these situations using a chance tree and the multiplication of chances. The area model is introduced as another model that can be used to find chances for a situation with two combined events.

Pacing and Planning

Day 15: The Game of Hog Again		Student pages 35–38
INTRODUCTION	Problems 1–3	Convert a tree diagram for rolling three number cubes into a chance tree.
CLASSWORK	Problem 4	Reflect on the differences between a tree diagram and a chance tree.
HOMEWORK	Problem 5	Evaluate a decision using the concepts of probability and expected value.

Day 16: A School Club Meeting		Student pages 38–41
INTRODUCTION	Problems 6 and 7	Use an area model to find the chance that two girls can go to a meeting.
CLASSWORK	Problems 8–10	Use a chance tree to model a situation and reason about the chance that three students are selected to go to a meeting.
HOMEWORK	Problems 11 and 12	Use chance trees and an area model to find chances for several multi-event situations.

Day 17: Summary		Student pages 42–44
INTRODUCTION	Review homework.	Review homework from Day 16.
CLASSWORK	Check Your Work For Further Reflection	Student self-assessment: Use chance trees, area models, and counting strategies to find probabilities for various situations.
HOMEWORK	Unit Review	Review Summary for Sections A–D.

Additional Resources: Additional Practice, Section D, Student Book page 50

Materials

Student Resources

No resources required

Teachers' Resources

No resources required

Student Materials

No material required

*See Hints and Comments for optional materials.

Learning Lines

Theoretical Chance

In this section, students revisit several situations with combined events from Section C. In Section C, students used experiments and simulations to find experimental probabilities. In this section, they learn how to calculate the theoretical chances for combined events. Several concepts are reinforced, including the inherent variability in the results of an experiment and the need for many trials for experimental chances to approach theoretical chances.

Models and Tools

The tree diagram is converted into a chance tree.

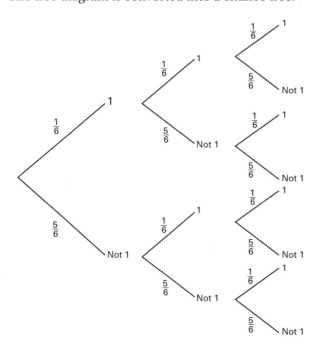

With a chance tree, it is not possible to count the endpoints to find all possible outcomes. Favorable outcomes cannot be "counted" either. However, routes for favorable outcomes can still be followed through the diagram to compute probabilities. Each route is labeled with the chance for a given outcome. Instead of counting routes and using the ratio of favorable outcomes to possible outcomes, chances are directly found by multiplying the chances along the route. The multiplication rule for chance is further formalized in the unit *Great Predictions*.

The area model is also introduced in this section as another way to find chances for two combined or successive events. Using an area model, students divide a rectangle or square in two directions to represent the number of outcomes for each event. The area of the whole rectangle represents a chance of 1, while the areas of the (un)shaded parts represent chances for the different outcomes as well as combined outcomes. Students can find chances as a ratio of the number of small units for a given part divided by the total number of small units in the rectangle. They can also multiply the lengths and widths (fractions) representing chances for each outcome.

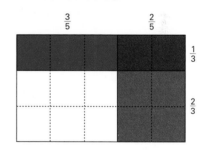

Expected Value

The idea of expected value is explored further using the game of Hog. Expected value is not yet formalized; however, students focus on the expected score to determine which group of number cubes might produce the best score.

At the End of the Section: Learning Outcomes

Students can make a chance tree or an area model to represent a combined event situation. They can also calculate chances for combined events using the multiplication rule. Students can express these chances as fractions, ratios, decimals, or percents.

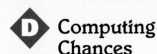

Computing Chances

Ask students about various games they have played involving cubes labeled with letters, numbers, or symbols.

Computing Chances

The Game of Hog Again

Sometimes you are concerned about the chance of more than one event happening. You might want to know the chances of first one thing and then another or maybe the chance of several things happening at the same time. How can you find the chance of a **combined event**?

For example, with the game of Hog you know that the chance of rolling a 1 with one number cube is one out of six, or $\frac{1}{6}$. But what about getting none, one, or two 1s when tossing two number cubes? Or more number cubes?

Akio is playing Hog and has rolled three number cubes.

Reaching All Learners

Extension

Students may find it interesting to explore the letter frequency for the set of "letter cubes" included with popular word games.

Hints and Comments

Overview

Students read about combined events in the introduction to this section. There are no problems on this page for students to solve.

About the Mathematics

For combined events, theoretical chances can be calculated if the chances are known for each of the single events involved. In the previous Probability unit *Take a Chance* and in Sections A through C of this unit, students solved simple problems involving chances for combined events or sequences of events. Students solved these problems using tree diagrams or tables to structure and model the situation, which made it easy to count the numbers of favorable and possible outcomes. In this section, the tree diagram is converted into a chance tree.

◆ **D** Computing
   Chances

Notes

1a Students need to begin the diagram and list some of the outcomes.

2 If students have difficulty, ask them what "not 1" means. *What number can be rolled if the outcome is "not 1?"*

Aiko wants to find the chance of not throwing a 1 with three number cubes. He decides to use a tree diagram to do this. This is part of his tree diagram.

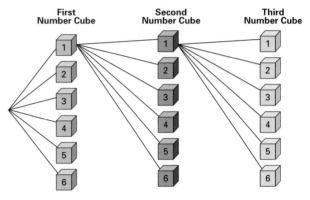

1. **a.** Describe what Akio's complete tree diagram for rolling three number cubes will look like. Note: You do not have to draw the complete diagram.

   b. Describe how you could use the complete tree diagram to find the chance of rolling no 1s with three number cubes.

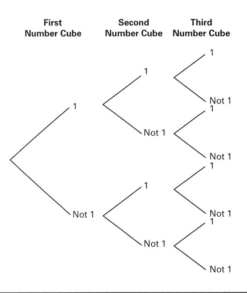

Celia thinks Akio can use a simpler tree diagram since the only important outcomes are "1" or "not 1." She suggests using a diagram like this.

2. Explain what Celia did to make this tree.

Reaching All Learners

Hands-On Learning

Roll three different-colored number cubes (or one number cube three times). List each outcome and discuss where they would fall on the tree diagram or on the chart.

Intervention

For problem 1, if students do not "see" what the tree diagram will look like, ask them to draw it and then describe how they completed the drawing.

How many total outcomes are there for throwing three cubes? Refer to the outfit activity on pages 1 and 2 in Section A.

Solutions and Samples

1. a. The complete tree diagram for rolling three number cubes would look messy, crowded, and cluttered. It would have, at first, six branches: one for each possible result of the first number cube. Each of those branches would have six branches for the second number cube. So there would be 36 endpoints. Each of these endpoints would also have six branches attached for each possible outcome of the third number cube. So overall, there would be $36 \times 6 = 216$ endpoints.

b. You can use the complete tree diagram to find the chance that no 1s are rolled by counting the paths along the branches of the tree where no 1s occur. These are the favorable outcomes. The number of favorable outcomes divided by the total outcomes possible, 216, gives the expected chance. If students count up the branches with no 1s, they will find 125 of these branches. So the theoretical chance of rolling no 1s with three number cubes is 125 out of 216, or 58%.

2. Celia made this tree by combining the five branches for rolling a 2, 3, 4, 5, or 6 and grouping them as one branch for "not rolling a 1."

Hints and Comments

Overview

Students study how a tree diagram for rolling three number cubes can be made into a simpler diagram called a *chance tree*.

About the Mathematics

For modeling complex situations involving sequences of events or combined events, a tree diagram is often too complex to draw. Instead, a chance tree may be used to represent and structure the situation and calculate chances. Each branch in a chance tree may represent several "outcomes" (like rolling a 2, 3, 4, 5, or 6). The chance on the outcome(s) represented by each branch is written next to that branch. The total number of outcomes and the number of favorable outcomes cannot be found in a chance tree by counting the routes. Instead, chances can be found by multiplying chances written in the tree.

Planning

Students may work on problems 1 and 2 individually or in pairs. Discuss problem 2 in class.

Comments About the Solutions

1. b. Students must understand what the favorable outcomes are and how to find these in the tree diagram.

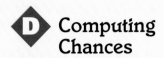

Computing Chances

Notes

3 This problem is crucial for understanding the relation between the chance tree and the underlying situation that is modeled by the chance tree. Discuss Josh's and Celia's statements separately.

Josh says, "There is only one route in this tree with 'not 1' for each number cube, so the chance of rolling 'not 1s' with three number cubes is one out of eight."

Celia says,"No, Josh, I don't think so. There are actually 5 × 5 × 5 or 125 routes that do not have a '1' in them."

3. a. Is Josh wrong? Explain your thinking.

   b. Explain how Celia reasoned to find that there are 5 × 5 × 5 routes for "not 1" with any of the number cubes.

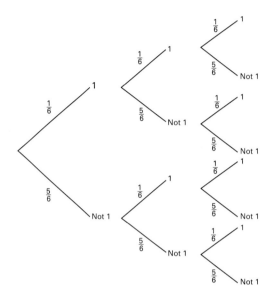

If you want Celia's tree diagram to be easily understood, some extra information is needed. This makes the tree diagram into a **chance tree**.

4d Note that the chances for rolling three 1s and three "not 1s" are not complementary chances. The other possible outcomes are combinations in which either one or two 1s are rolled. This can easily be seen in the chance tree. Discuss why the multiplication rule works and how it relates to the chance tree.

4. a. Reflect What is the difference between a tree diagram and a chance tree?

   b. Use the chance tree to explain that the chance of rolling three 1s with three number cubes is $\frac{1}{6} \times \frac{1}{6} \times \frac{1}{6}$.

   c. Write the chance of rolling three 1s as a decimal.

   d. Calculate the chance of rolling "not 1s" with three number cubes.

   e. Reflect Do you think choosing to roll three number cubes in the game of Hog is a good decision? Explain your thinking.

Assessment Pyramid

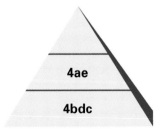

Use chance trees to find probability.

Make decisions using probability and expected values.

Reaching All Learners

Vocabulary Building

Have students write definitions and give examples that distinguish the tree diagram and the chance tree.

Intervention

It may help students who find problem 4b difficult to think about what the tree diagram would look like and how they would find the chance then: there are 6 × 6 × 6 possible outcomes, one of which is the favorable one, so the chance on this is 1 out of 216, which is $\frac{1}{216}$.

Solutions and Samples

3. a. Yes, Josh is wrong. Sample explanation:

There are actually five out of six branches represented by the "not 1" branch. Not rolling a 1 means rolling either a 2, 3, 4, 5, or 6.

b. Celia uses the fact that each of the branches for "not 1" actually is five additional branches (see answer to **3a**). So she counts the path marked completely with "not 1" as $5 \times 5 \times 5$ branches.

4. a. Answers will vary. Sample answer:

A tree diagram has a branch for each possible outcome. All possible outcomes have an equal chance. There is no need to label each branch with a percent or fraction. With a tree diagram you find the chance for a combination of events by counting the favorable paths (or outcomes) and dividing this by the number of all possible paths (or outcomes).

A chance tree has a branch for every relevant outcome. Each outcome may be a combination of several outcomes. For example, the outcome "not rolling 1" is a combination of the outcomes for rolling either a 2, 3, 4, 5, or 6. The outcomes represented by the branches do not need to have the same chance. Therefore, it is necessary to label the branches of the chance tree with the chance for each type of event.

b. The chance of rolling three 1s with three number cubes is $\frac{1}{6} \times \frac{1}{6} \times \frac{1}{6}$. This can be found by following the path through the chance tree where the branch ends with a 1. You then multiply the chance for each branch.

c. The chance of rolling three 1s is 1 out of 216. This is about 0.005, or 0.5% (that is, half of 1%).

d. The chance of "no 1s" can be found by following the paths along the "not 1" branches. This is $\frac{5}{6} \times \frac{5}{6} \times \frac{5}{6}$, which is 125 out of 216; this is about 0.579, which is about 58%.

e. Answers may vary. Sample answers:

- Yes, choosing to roll three number cubes in the game of Hog is a clever decision because the chance that you will roll "no 1s" is almost 60%. This is more than $\frac{1}{2}$, and you can get more points if you roll three number cubes.

- No, this is not a clever decision. You still have at least a 40% chance to roll a 1, and you do not get very many points with just three number cubes.

Hints and Comments

Overview

Students continue their exploration of the chance tree for rolling three number cubes. They reason about the difference between a tree diagram and a chance tree and are introduced to the multiplication rule for probability.

About the Mathematics

In a chance tree, the chances are written with the branches and the outcomes are at the "nodes" or the end of the branches. A route can be followed by choosing the appropriate branch (fitting the problem that must be solved) at each node. The chance on that particular outcome (via that route) is the product of the chances along the chosen branches. If the chances along the branches are written as fractions, the not-simplified fraction that is the product has "number of favorable outcomes" as the numerator and "the number of all possible outcomes" as the denominator. This is the same as in the formula students have seen before.

Chance trees can also be used to model situations in which the chances are not directly based on countable outcomes. For example, to find the chance to randomly pick the letter "r" from a text twice in a row, you cannot make a tree diagram in which each branch represents one letter in which you can count the number of outcomes. However, a chance tree with the chances listed along the branches can be made.

Planning

Students may work on problem 3 individually or in pairs. You may want to discuss problem 3 before having students complete problem 4.

Comments About the Problems

4. a. Make sure students understand the difference.

e. Some students will answer this based solely on their answer to problem 4d. They should recognize that the trade off is between the chance of getting at least a one (which is about 40%) and the chance of getting a large score. To find out how big the expected or average score is with three number cubes, students may use their results from the game of Hog they played in the previous section.

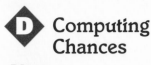

Computing Chances

Notes

6 Remind students to write these as fractions.

5. **a.** Investigate the chance of rolling "not 1s" for another number of number cubes in Hog.

   b. If you want the biggest chance of not getting a "1," how many number cubes should you roll? Explain your reasoning.

   c. If you want to get a big score, how many number cubes do you think you should roll? Explain your reasoning.

A School Club Meeting

Sonia and Aysa are cousins. They both live in Middletown, but they go to different middle schools. Both Sonia and Aysa are members of the committee that organizes the clubs at their respective schools. All middle schools in Middletown will send representatives from their club committees to a citywide meeting.

Sonia's committee has five students. Two of them can go to the meeting.

Aysa's committee has three students and will send one of them to the meeting.

The two committees decide to select at random the students who will go to the meeting.

6. **a.** What is the chance that Sonia will be selected?

   b. What is the chance that Aysa will be selected?

Sonia wonders what the chance is that both she and Aysa can go to the meeting. To find out, she makes a diagram.

First she draws a rectangle.

Assessment Pyramid

6ab

Use different representations to describe probability.

Reaching All Learners

Intervention

Ask students how many outcomes for two cubes? (36) Three cubes? (216) This will help them separate how to get the denominator from the numerator for their chance statements.

Solutions and Samples

5. a. Answers will vary, depending on the number of number cubes students chose. Sample answer for 4 number cubes:

The chance of not rolling ones is $\frac{5}{6} \times \frac{5}{6} \times \frac{5}{6} \times \frac{5}{6}$. This is about 0.48, which is 48%. I found this by extending the pattern in the chance tree.

The table below outlines the chance for rolling "not 1s" for one through eight number cubes:

Number of Cubes	Calculation for Rolling No Ones	Chance of Rolling No Ones
1	$\frac{5}{6}$	83%
2	$\frac{5}{6} \times \frac{5}{6}$	69%
3	$\frac{5}{6} \times \frac{5}{6} \times \frac{5}{6}$	58%
4	$\frac{5}{6} \times \frac{5}{6} \times \frac{5}{6} \times \frac{5}{6}$	48%
5	$\frac{5}{6} \times \frac{5}{6} \times \frac{5}{6} \times \frac{5}{6} \times \frac{5}{6}$	40%
6	$\frac{5}{6} \times \frac{5}{6} \times \frac{5}{6} \times \frac{5}{6} \times \frac{5}{6} \times \frac{5}{6}$	33%
7	$\frac{5}{6} \times \frac{5}{6} \times \frac{5}{6} \times \frac{5}{6} \times \frac{5}{6} \times \frac{5}{6} \times \frac{5}{6}$	28%
8	$\frac{5}{6} \times \frac{5}{6} \times \frac{5}{6} \times \frac{5}{6} \times \frac{5}{6} \times \frac{5}{6} \times \frac{5}{6} \times \frac{5}{6}$	23%

b. If you only want the best chance of not getting a 1, you should roll one number cube. The chance of not rolling a 1 with one cube is 83%.

c. Answers will vary, depending on the way someone decides between the chance of rolling at least one 1 and getting a score of 0, with the potential score if no 1s are rolled. Sample responses:

- Three number cubes, because you have over a 50% chance of not getting a 1, and you can score more points.

- One or two number cubes, because the fewer number cubes you roll, the lower the chance you will roll a 1 and get no points.

6. a. The chance Sonia will be selected to go the meeting is 2 out of 5, which is $\frac{2}{5}$, or 40%.

b. The chance Aysa will be selected is $\frac{1}{3}$.

Hints and Comments

Overview

Student investigate the theoretical chance of rolling "no 1s" for different numbers of number cubes in the game of Hog. They use chance trees and apply the multiplication rule. Students also discuss a situation in which students are randomly selected to go to a school club meeting and reason about the chances for particular students to be selected.

About the Mathematics

The chance tree used to structure and model a situation for finding the chance on not rolling 1s with three number cubes can easily be extended to find the similar chance for four or more number cubes. Often sketching a chance tree may help structure the situation; in that case, it is not necessary to draw the complete tree. Instead of drawing the extra branches to the tree, students may also reason about the calculation involved and use multiplication of chances.

Note that the chance tree for the combined event of rolling several number cubes at the same time is the same as the chance tree for rolling the same number cube several times (a sequence of events). The rolling of a number cube is independent of the rolling of other number cubes.

Planning

Student can work on problem 5 individually or in pairs.

Comments About the Solutions

5. If students have problems, refer them to problem 4d, on page 37. Some students may prefer to draw the chance tree; this can be done for smaller numbers. For larger numbers, encourage them to just sketch the branches they need and look for the pattern in the calculations. Other students may use the multiplication of chances without drawing the tree. In a class discussion, you can collect students answers and find the chances for all numbers of number cubes used in the game of Hog. (See Solutions and Samples column.)

c. Make sure students now take into account both the score they can get as well as the chance of not rolling 1s. If students have no idea about the scores, they may want to look back at the results of the games of Hog played in class (see Student Book page 30).

D Computing Chances

Notes

Have students draw the area model and label each area.

Ask why Sonia split the rectangle into five vertical parts and three horizontal parts.

She divides it in five equal vertical strips and shades two of the strips.

She divides the whole rectangle in three equal horizontal strips and shades one. Note that she has to shade all the way across.

Finally she writes some fractions with the diagram.

  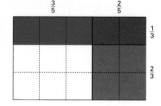

7. a Explain how each of Sonia's diagrams relates to finding the chance that both of them will go to the meeting.

b. What is the chance that both Sonia and Aysa will go? How did you find this chance?

c. What is the chance that neither of them will go to the meeting?

7c Make sure students realize that the outcomes "both will go" and "neither will go" are not complementary. This can clearly be seen in the drawings.

After problems 7abc, ask students what the chance is of only one of the girls being chosen.

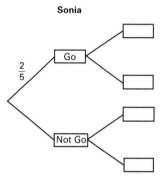

The rectangle Sonia drew to help her figure out the chance is called an **area model**. You can also use a chance tree to calculate the chance that both Sonia and Aysa will be selected to go to the meeting.

Here you see the beginning of the chance tree you might use.

8 Have students compare their answers for **7b** and **8b** as well as their methods for finding the answers.

8. a. Copy the chance tree and finish it.

b. Calculate the chance that both Sonia and Aysha will go to the meeting. Write the chance as a fraction as well as a percentage.

c. What is the chance that only one of them will go to the meeting? Write the chance as a fraction as well as a percentage. Explain how you found this chance.

Assessment Pyramid

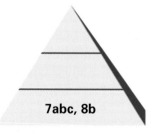

7abc, 8b

Find the possible outcomes for various situations.

Use area models to find probability.

Reaching All Learners

Intervention

For problem 7b, you may need to ask, *How many small squares are in this area model?* (15) *How many shaded squares represent both girls attending?* (2) *What is the chance?* ($\frac{2}{15}$).

If students have difficulty answering problem 7c, prompt them to indicate the area representing the chance that neither student will go in the area model.

Solutions and Samples

7. a. Sonia's diagram is a rectangle that is vertically divided into 5 parts (or columns), where the right two columns represent a chance of $\frac{2}{5}$ that Sonia is going to the meeting. This can be seen in the first drawing above problem 7. The rectangle is then divided horizontally into three parts (or rows), where the upper shaded part represents the chance of $\frac{1}{3}$ that Aysa will go to the meeting. This can be seen in the second drawing. In the last drawing, the model is labeled with these chances, and the part that is shaded twice (the upper right part) represents the chance that both Aysa and Sonia will go to the meeting.

b. The chance both Sonia and Aysa will go to the meeting is indicated by the part that is shaded twice (in the upper right corner). It represents a chance of $\frac{2}{15}$. This can be found by either counting all the small squares in the rectangle that were shaded twice and dividing by the total number of squares, or students can multiply the fractions that represent the shaded part of the rectangle's length and width $\frac{2}{5} \times \frac{1}{3}$.

c. The chance that neither of them will go to the meeting is represented by the large, unshaded area in the lower left corner. This chance is $\frac{6}{15}$ (or $\frac{2}{5}$).

8. a.

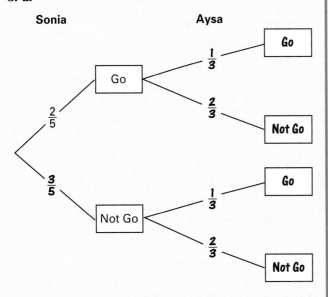

b. The chance both Sonia and Aysa will go to the meeting is $\frac{2}{5} \times \frac{1}{3} = \frac{2}{15}$, which is about 13%.

c. The chance only one of them will go to the meeting is the chance that Sonia will go and Aysa will not ($\frac{2}{5} \times \frac{2}{3} = \frac{4}{15}$), plus the chance that Sonia will not go and that Aysa will go ($\frac{3}{5} \times \frac{1}{3} = \frac{3}{15}$). So the chance that only one of them will go is $\frac{7}{15}$, or about 47%.

Hints and Comments

Overview

Students are introduced to the area model, which can be used to organize the school club meeting problem.

About the Mathematics

An area model can be used to find chances for situations involving two combined events. To create an area model, a rectangle or square is drawn (the dimensions are not important). The rectangle is then divided into equal vertical strips that represent the equally likely outcomes for the first event. Using the example on this page, each vertical strip would represent a student randomly selected from the first committee. The number of strips representing favorable outcomes are shaded. In the example, two out of five students from the committee will be selected; so two vertical strips are shaded. The same type of partitioning is done horizontally for the second event.

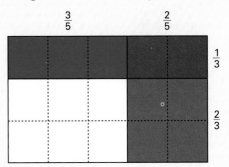

The portion of the area model shaded twice represents the chance that both girls can go. The area can either be expressed as the ratio of shaded units to the total number of units: 2 out of 15. Or the area can also be calculated by multiplying the probability for each event, written as fractions. Students used the area model in the Geometry and Measurement unit *Reallotment* for calculating areas.

Planning

You may want to discuss the process of drawing the area model with the whole class. Following this discussion, students can work individually on problem 7.

Comments About the Solutions

8. Students now must use the multiplication rule to find the chance that both Sonia and Aysa will go. It is not possible to just count endpoints or routes.

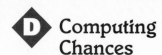

Sonia and Aysa have a friend named Dani. Dani is also on the club committee at his middle school.

Four students are on his committee, and one of them will be sent to the meeting to represent the committee.

9a You may want to remind students about the For Further Reflection problem at the end of Section B (page 22), where they had to compare the use of a tree diagram to the use of a two-way table.

9. **a.** Can you use the area model to find the chance that Sonia, Aysa, and Dani will all be sent to the meeting? If so, show how to do this. If not, explain why not.

   b. Can you use the chance tree to find this chance? If so, show how to do this. If not, explain why not.

Tests

9b Have students draw or sketch the chance tree.

In Section C, you explored the chances of guessing correctly on a true-false test by flipping a coin. You estimated the chance based on a simulation. In this case, you can also calculate the theoretical chance.

10a You may point out to students that this chance tree has a similar layout as the tree diagram for families with three children from Section A. Instead of using labels G and B, C (correct), and I (incorrect or wrong) are used. Because both the chances are equal ($\frac{1}{2}$), the tree diagram and the chance tree are similar for this situation.

10. **a.** Make a chance tree that you can use to calculate the chance of getting three true-false questions correct by guessing.

   b. Use the tree you made for part **a** to find the following chances.

   • The chance that two out of the three questions are answered correctly.

   • The chance that all questions are answered incorrectly.

   • The chance that at least one of the questions is answered correctly.

In Section C, you worked on problems about Charlie who took a geography test consisting of ten statements that are either true or false.

Select the best answer.

Sydney is the capital of Australia.

○ True
○ False

Assessment Pyramid

9ab

Understand the limitations of various models used to find probability.

Reaching All Learners

Intervention

Students may need additional practice converting fractions to percents. Several practice worksheets to reinforce student knowledge of rational numbers can be found in the *Number Tools* resource.

If students have difficulty answering problem 10b, have them trace the paths in their tree diagram that result in the described outcome.

Extension

Have students create an area model to find the chance of rolling a 1 (or "not 1") when rolling two number cubes.

Solutions and Samples

9. a. No, the area model cannot be used because you would need an extra dimension to include the chance for Dani.

b. Yes, you can use the chance tree to find this chance by extending the tree. Each endpoint gets two extra branches for Dani: Go with chance $\frac{1}{4}$ and not go with chance $\frac{3}{4}$.

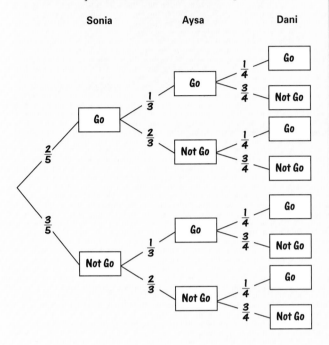

The chance that all three will go is $\frac{2}{5} \times \frac{1}{3} \times \frac{1}{4} = \frac{2}{60}$, which is about 3%.

10. a.

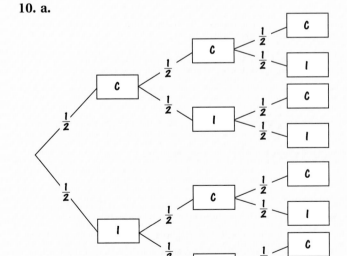

Hints and Comments

Overview

Students further explore the context of the school club meeting. They use a chance tree to model the situation. Students reason about the chance that three randomly students, each from a different committee, will be selected to go to the meeting.

About the Mathematics

In situations with two combined events (or in sequence), both a chance tree and an area model can be used to reason about and calculate chances. If more than two events occur, the area model cannot be used in the same way as shown on the previous page since it has only two dimensions. In Section B, students were asked to reflect on a similar problem, comparing the use of a two-way table to a tree diagram (see the For Further Reflection problem on page 22).

Planning

Students can work on problem 9 individually or in pairs. Share students' solutions in class.

b.

- The chance that two out of the three questions are answered correctly is the sum of the chances along the routes CCI and CIC and ICC. Each of these has the same chance of occurring: $\frac{1}{2} \times \frac{1}{2} \times \frac{1}{2} = \frac{1}{8}$. So the chance of getting two questions out of three correct is $3 \times \frac{1}{8} = \frac{3}{8}$, or 37.5%.

- The chance that all questions are answered incorrectly is the chance of III, which is $\frac{1}{2} \times \frac{1}{2} \times \frac{1}{2} = \frac{1}{8}$, or 12.5%.

- The chance that at least one question is answered correctly is $\frac{7}{8}$, or 87.5 %. Note: This is not the same as correctly answering exactly one question. To find the chance of getting **at least** one question correct, you need to find the chance of getting 1, 2, or all 3 questions correct. This can be calculated in two ways: a) the chances for each route with at least one C can be added together, or b) you can find the chance of incorrectly answering all of the questions and subtracting this from 1 (or 100%). The chance of incorrectly answering all of the questions is $\frac{1}{8}$. So $1 - \frac{1}{8} = \frac{7}{8}$, or 87.5 %.

D Computing Chances

Notes

11 Refer students back to the Section C simulation of the ten-question test.

Charlie guessed the answers to all questions. He will pass the test if he got at least seven answers correct.

11. a. Describe what a chance tree for the geography test that Charlie took by guessing would look like. Note: You do not need to draw the whole chance tree, but you may want to draw a part of it.

b. What is the chance that Charlie will guess all 10 questions correctly? How did you calculate this chance?

As part of a test, Jamie needs to answer two multiple-choice questions. Each question has three possible answers, labeled A, B, and C.

Jamie says, "Last time, I guessed all the answers and did not pass the test. I think I can do better this time."

12. a. Use a chance tree to find the chance that Jamie will guess both questions correctly.

b. What is the chance that Jamie will guess only one of the two questions correctly?

c. Describe an easy way to find the chance that Jamie will guess both questions incorrectly.

d. Reflect Is it possible to use the area model to find these chances? If yes, show how. If no, explain why not.

12a Students may also draw a tree with three branches for each question: one branch for Correct and two branches for Incorrect. All of these branches would then have the same chance of $\frac{1}{3}$.

12c Discuss how complementary chances can be used to solve this problem.

Assessment Pyramid

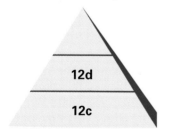

12d

12c

Understand the limitations of various models used to find probability.

Use complementary probability.

Reaching All Learners

Intervention

For problem 11, it is important that students understand the structure of the chance tree and know how to use the chance tree to calculate probabilities. It may be helpful to draw part of the tree, or partly extend the tree from problem 10 by drawing new branches for "C" and "I" at each endpoint until the tree has split into branches ten times.

Solutions and Samples

11. a. A chance tree for the geography test Charlie takes by guessing will have ten "columns," one for each question. At each node there are two branches: one for Correct and one for Incorrect. Since this is a chance tree, both of these branches should be labeled with the chance $\frac{1}{2}$.

Sample response: It would look like the tree for problem 10a, but it would have branches for seven more questions.

b. The chance is 0.00097, which is about 0.1%, or 1 out of 1000.

Sample calculation: There is only one route that represents Charlie correctly guessing all 10 questions. This is route CCCCCCCCCC. The chance for this route is $\frac{1}{2} \times \frac{1}{2} \times \cdots \times \frac{1}{2} = (\frac{1}{2})^{10}$. This is 0.00097, which is about 0.1%, or 1 out of 1000 times.

12. a. The chance tree will look like this:

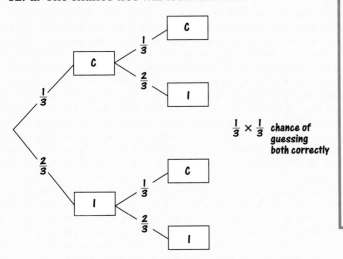

$\frac{1}{3} \times \frac{1}{3}$ chance of guessing both correctly

The chance that Jamie answers both questions correctly is $\frac{1}{3} \times \frac{1}{3} = \frac{1}{9}$, which is about 11%.

b. About 44%. Explanation: Guessing only one of the two questions correctly can happen in two ways: CI and IC (see chance tree for part **a**). The chance for each of these outcomes is $\frac{1}{3} \times \frac{2}{3} = \frac{2}{9}$, which is about 22%. So the chance of guessing only one question correctly is double this, or about 44%.

c. The chance that Jamie guesses both questions incorrectly is what is left from 100% after subtracting the chance for answering both questions correctly (from part **a**) and for answering one question correctly (from part **b**). So the chance of incorrectly guessing on both questions is 100% − 11% − 44% = 45%.

Hints and Comments

Overview

Students use chance trees and an area model to find chances for multi-event situations. They use the multiplication rule and complementary chances to find probabilities for several outcomes.

About the Mathematics

Students solve chance problems using what they have learned so far in this section about calculating theoretical chances for multi-event situations.

Planning

Students may work individually or in pairs to complete the problems on this page.

d. Yes, the area model may be used.

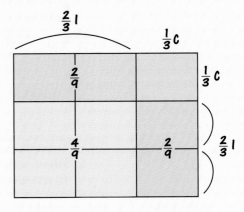

The area of the double shaded part in the upper right represents the chance of having both questions correct, which is $\frac{1}{3} \times \frac{1}{3} = \frac{1}{9}$.

Summary ▶◀

To find if the chance that an event will occur in different ways, you can collect data from a survey. Sometimes you can compute the theoretical chance of an event.

Chance: If all possible outcomes are equally likely, the chance that an event will occur is the number of successful outcomes divided by the number of possible outcomes.

With a chance tree, you can calculate chances for combined events. To find the theoretical chance, you have to carefully count the possibilities in which you are interested.

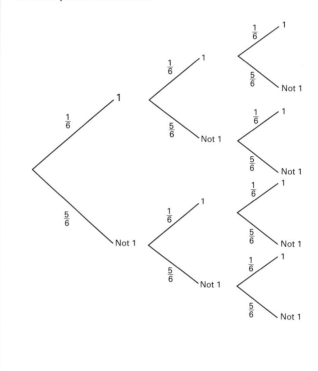

Reaching All Learners

Vocabulary Building

This Summary section contains many key terms used to describe probability: *chance, theoretical, successful outcomes, possible outcomes, combined events, chance tree,* and *area model.* Students should make sure their notebook includes all of these terms with descriptions and examples, as needed.

Hints and Comments

Overview

Students read the Summary, which reviews the main concepts covered in this section.

Sometimes an area model can be used to solve a chance problem about combined events.

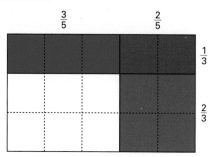

The advantage of a chance tree over an area model is that you can combine more than just two outcomes.

Check Your Work

1. **a.** Use the chance tree for the game of Hog, in problem 3 of this section, to calculate the chance of rolling two 1s with three number cubes. Write the chance as a fraction and as a percent.

   b. What is the chance, as a percentage, of rolling "not 1s" with six number cubes in the game of Hog?

2. Mr. and Mrs. Lewis have four daughters. You may assume that the chance of having a son is the same as having a daughter: $\frac{1}{2}$. Comment on each of the following statements.

   a. The chance that their next child is a girl is smaller than $\frac{1}{2}$ because a family with five daughters is very unlikely.

   b. The chance is one half because the chance of a girl is $\frac{1}{2}$.

   c. The chance is larger than $\frac{1}{2}$ because the Lewises apparently have a tendency to have girls.

Assessment Pyramid

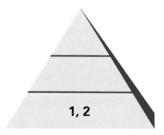

1, 2

Assesses Section D Goals

Reaching All Learners

Intervention

You may need to refer some students back to the approaches used with "three child families," investigated in Section A.

Solutions and Samples

Answers to Check Your Work

1. **a.** The chance of rolling two 1s with three number cubes is $3 \times \frac{1}{6} \times \frac{1}{6} \times \frac{5}{6}$, which is about 7%. You can find this chance by following the paths in the chance tree that have two 1s and one "not 1." The chance of each of these outcomes is $\frac{1}{6} \times \frac{1}{6} \times \frac{5}{6}$, and there are three such paths.

   b. The chance of rolling no 1s with six number cubes in the game of Hog is $\frac{5}{6} \times \frac{5}{6} \times \frac{5}{6} \times \frac{5}{6} \times \frac{5}{6} \times \frac{5}{6}$, or $(\frac{5}{6})^6 = 33\%$. You can think about how a chance tree for six number cubes would look by extending the one from problem three. You then follow the path along the "not 1s" and multiply the chances.

2. **a.** This statement is not true. The chance that their next child is a girl is still $\frac{1}{2}$ because for each child the chance that it is a boy is the same as the chance that it is a girl. For a family to have five daughters seems unlikely, but it is $(\frac{1}{2})^5$, or $\frac{1}{32}$, which is about 3%, so about three out of every 100 families with five children are likely to have five girls.

   b. This statement is true.

   c. "The chance is larger than $\frac{1}{2}$ because the Lewises apparently have a tendency to have girls." If you believe that the chance of having a boy is the same as the chance of having a girl, this would not be true.

Hints and Comments

Overview

Students complete Check Your Work problems as a self-assessment of key concepts and skills from this section. Students can check their answers on Student Book pages 55 and 56.

Planning

After students complete Section D, you may assign as homework appropriate activities from the Additional Practice section. These problems are located on Student Book page 50.

Computing
Chances

Remember Sonia and Dani from problems 6–9 in this section?
Sonia's committee has 5 students, and two of them can go to the
meeting. Dani's committee has 4 students, and one of them will be
sent to the meeting to represent the committee.

3. Use the area model to calculate the chance that both Sonia and
Dani will go to the meeting.

River Middle School has lockers with three-digit codes. The school
wants to install lockers with two-letter codes.

4. a. Are there more combinations with three digits or with two
letters?

b. If you were in charge at a school, would you choose lockers
with three digits or two letters, assuming that they have the
same quality and price? Explain your reasoning.

c. Mae is a student at River Middle School and does not have
her two-letter code yet. What is the chance that she will get RR
as her code?

For Further Reflection

Describe the different ways you have used to find the chance of an
event in all of the sections in Second Chance. Can you use any way
you want for any situation? Explain why or why not.

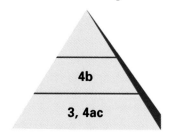

Assessment Pyramid

4b

3, 4ac

Assesses Section D Goals

Reaching All Learners

Study Skills

The For Further Reflection problem is a good opportunity for students to
review what they have learned in this unit. Have students prepare a
summary outline of different models and techniques they used. For each
model or technique, have students give examples and describe situations
in which these models can and cannot be applied.

Solutions and Samples

Hints and Comments

3. The chance that both Dani and Sonia will go is represented by the two purple squares. The chance is 2 out of 20, which is $\frac{1}{10}$, or 10%. You can also find this chance by calculating: $\frac{2}{5} \times \frac{1}{4} = \frac{2}{20} = \frac{1}{10}$.

In this calculation, $\frac{2}{5}$ is the chance that Sonia can go and $\frac{1}{4}$ is the chance that Dani can go.

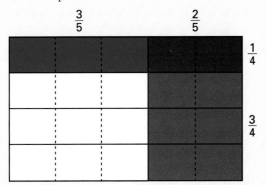

4. a. If you write the two-letter code like this __–__, you can make 26 × 26 = 676 combinations. Because the alphabet has 26 letters, you can choose one to fill in the first space, and you can fill in the second blank with any letter, so the total is 26 × 26.

With three numbers, the code can be written like this: __–__–__. For each "place," you can choose from 10 digits (0, 1, 2, 3, 4, 5, 6, 7, 8, 9), so there are 10 × 10 × 10 = 1,000 possible codes. This is more then 676, so there are more three-number codes.

b. Different answers are possible and correct. Be sure to give a good reason for your choice. You may want to discuss your solutions with your classmates. What you choose may depend on the number of students and lockers. If 676 lockers is enough, you can choose a two-letter code. You may want to have more lockers later and prefer the three-digit code. You may also consider what is easier for the students to remember, three digits or two letters.

c. If the codes are assigned at random from all possible two-letter codes, the chance that Mae will get RR as her code is 1 out of 676; this is about 0.0015, or 0.15%.

Overview

Students continue completing the Check Your Work and For Further Reflection problems for Section D.

For Further Reflection

Answers will vary. The methods for finding chances can be found in the Summaries.

Sample answer:

> We used tree diagrams, charts, and tables like two-way tables, rules, chance trees, an area model and calculations. We found and used theoretical chances and also used relative frequencies to calculate experimental chances. These were based on information collected in surveys or experiments. We also found chances doing simulations. Not all methods can always be used. For example the two-way table and the area model can only be used for situations with two events. A tree diagram can only be used if all outcomes are equally likely otherwise you can use a chance tree.

Additional Practice

Section Ⓐ Make a Choice

1. To decide whether to play the game Hilary wants to play or the game Robert wants to play, they toss a coin three times. They will play the game Hillary wants if there are exactly two heads.

   a. Do you think this is a fair way of deciding?

   b. How many different outcomes are possible? Explain your reasoning.

   c. Make a tree diagram of tossing three coins.

   d. What is the chance for the outcomes of tossing exactly two heads?

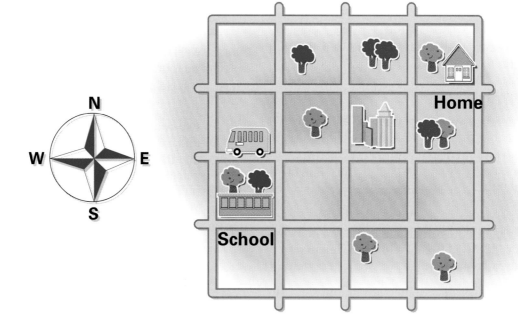

2. Robert walks home from school; both places are at the corner of two streets and the map looks like a grid.

   a. How many blocks north does Robert have to walk? And how many east?

   b. How many different routes can Robert take home from school?

Section A. Made a Choice

1. a. This is not a fair approach. There are fewer ways to get exactly two heads than to get the other outcomes. So Robert has a greater chance of choosing the game he wants to play. Note: If students give an incorrect answer for part **a**, they will have an opportunity to rethink their conjecture in parts **b** through **d**.

b. There are eight possible outcomes: HHH, HHT, HTH, THH, TTT, TTH, THT, HTT. Students may demonstrate their reasoning by making a list, making a tree diagram, or they may suggest that the tree diagram for having three children is the same as the one for tossing three coins.

c.

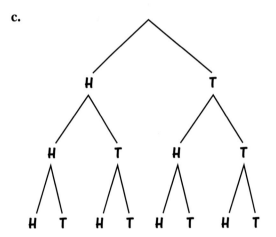

d. Use the definition of chance. Three outcomes have exactly two heads, and eight outcomes are possible. So the chance of getting exactly two heads is $\frac{3}{8}$.

2. a. Robert has to walk two blocks north and three blocks east.

Sample route:

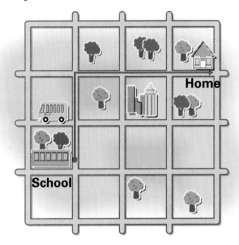

b. There are ten possible routes Robert can walk home:

NNEEE

NENEE

NEENE

NEEEN

EEENN

EENEN

ENEEN

ENENE

EENNE

ENNEE

(Note: Only the shortest routes are needed. All other routes are longer.)

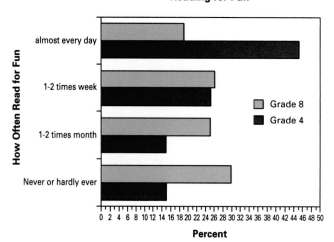

◆ **Additional Practice**

Section ⬥B A Matter of Information

Reading for Fun

This graph is based on the results of a survey about how often students from grades 4 and 8 read for fun.

Suppose you randomly pick a student from this survey from the fourth grade and one from the eighth grade.

Source: 2003 National Assessment of Educational Progress

1. **a** What is the chance that the eighth grade student will read almost every day?

   b. Compare the chances that each of them will read almost every day.

   c. Is the chance of the eighth grader reading less than once or twice a week greater than the chance the fourth grader doing the same? Explain how you found out.

2. The Edwards Middle School newspaper wanted to report on the grades of students who were band members. The results of a survey of everyone in the school are in the table.

	Average B or Higher	Average Less Than B	Total
Band Member	27	22	
Non-Band Member	115	108	
Total			

   a. Complete the table.

Section B. A Matter of Information

1. a. The chance that the eighth grade student will read almost every day is about 20%.

b. The chance that the fourth grade student will read almost every day is about 45%, which is much larger than the chance that the eighth grade student will read almost every day (20%). In fact, it is more than twice the chance.

c. The chance that the eighth grader will read less than 1–2 times a week is greater than the chance that the fourth grader will read less than 1–2 times a week. The bars for the eighth grader labeled "1–2 times a month" and "never or hardly ever" are longer than the corresponding bars for the fourth grader.

2. a.

	Average B or Higher	Average Less Than B	Total
Band Member	27	22	49
Non-Band Member	115	108	223
Total	142	130	272

b. A student is chosen at random from the school.

- What is the chance that the student is in the band?

- What is the chance that the student has a B or higher grade?

- What is the chance that the student is in the band and has a B or higher grade?

c. What is the chance that the student is in the band and has a grade less than a B?

d. Assuming the student is in the band, what is the chance that he or she has a grade less than a B?

e. What is the difference between the questions in parts **c** and **d**?.

3. A survey of 140 seventh grade students at Bell Middle School was given. These are some of the results.

- 62 of the students played video games two or more hours a day.

- 45 of the students played video games two or more hours a day and liked school.

- The chance that a randomly chosen student from the survey likes school is $\frac{2}{3}$.

	Like School	Do Not Like School	Total
Play Video Games 2 or More Hours a Day			
Play Video Games Less Than 2 Hours a Day			
Total			140

a. Copy and fill in the table with the correct numbers of students, using the results from the survey above.

b. What is the chance that a randomly chosen seventh grader plays video games less than two hours a day and likes school?

c. If you know that a student likes school, what is the chance that he or she plays video games less than two hours a day?

d. Explain how parts **b** and **c** are different.

b. The chance that a randomly chosen student from the school:

- will be in the band is $\frac{49}{272}$, or about 18%.

- will have an average grade of B or higher is $\frac{142}{272}$, or about 52%.

- will be in the band and have an average grade of B or higher is $\frac{27}{272}$, or about 10%.

c. The chance that the randomly chosen student is in the band and has an average grade less than B is $\frac{22}{272}$, or about 8%.

d. If you know the student is in the band, the chance that the student has an average grade less than B is $\frac{22}{49}$, or about 45%.

e. In part **c,** you compare the outcome to the total number of students. In part **d,** you only look at the total number of band members.

3 a.

	Like School	Do Not Like School	Total
Play Video Games 2 or More Hours a Day	**45** (first entry)	**17** ($= 47 - 30$, fourth entry)	**62** (first entry)
Play Video Games Less Than 2 Hours a Day	**48** ($= 93 - 45$, second entry)	**30** ($= 78 - 48$, third entry)	**78** ($= 140 - 62$, second entry)
Total	**93** ($= \frac{2}{3}$ of 140, second entry)	**47** ($= 140 - 93$, third entry)	**140** (first entry)

b. The chance that a randomly chosen seventh grade student plays video games less than 2 hours a day and likes school is $\frac{48}{140}$, or about 34%.

c. The chance that a student, who you know likes school, plays video games less than 2 hours a day is $\frac{48}{93}$, or about 52%.

d. Parts **b** and **c** are different. In part **b,** you consider all students. In part **c,** you only take into account the students who like school.

Additional Practice

Section ◆C◆ In the Long Run

A graphing calculator was used to simulate guessing the answers on a ten-question true-false test. The calculator simulated taking the test 500 times.

**500 Simulations of Guessing Answers
on a 10-Question True-False Test**

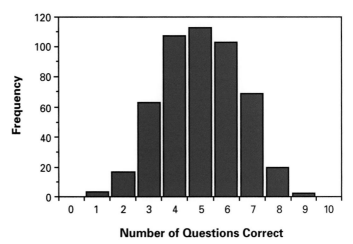

Number of Questions Correct

The graph shows the results of the simulation. You pass the test when seven or more out of the ten questions are correct.

1. a. What is the most likely outcome? Why do you think so?

    b. Estimate the chance that you would pass if "passing" were changed from 7 to 6 out of the 10 correct.

    c. Estimate the chance that you would get nine or more correct by guessing.

2. Sabrina has a 50% free-throw shooting percentage. She wants to know the chance that she has of making at least three free throws in the next eight shots she takes.

    a. Describe how she might use a simulation to help her find out.

    b. Would her chances of making at least three free throws in the next six tries be better than her chance of making at least three in the next eight tries? Why or why not?

Section C. In the Long Run

1. a. The most likely outcome is having 5 of the 10 questions correct. Sample answer: Because the chance is 50% for a correct answer and 50% for a wrong answer, you would expect half the answers to be correct and half to be incorrect.

b. The chance that you would pass, if the passing score was changed from seven to six out of ten correct is $\frac{100 + 70 + 20 + 3}{500}$. This is about 39%.

c. The chance you would get nine or more questions correct by guessing is about 3 out of 500, or about 0.6% (or about one half of 1%).

2. a. To find the chance that Sabrina has of making at least three free throws in the next eight shots she takes, since she has a 50% free throw shooting percentage, Sabrina can use a coin flip for a simulation. If she flips heads, then she makes the free throw; if she flips tails, then she misses the free throw. She can flip the coin eight times and record the results. She needs to repeat this "flipping the coin eight times" many times to find out how often she will make three or more out of eight free throws.

Comment: Instead of flipping a coin, Sabrina could use any other tool or device where two outcomes would have an equal chance. For example, a number cube can be used: the even numbers could represent "making the free throw," and the odd numbers could represent "missing the free throw."

b. Sabrina's chances of making at least three free throws in the next six tries are less than her chance of making at least three in the next eight tries. This is because in eight tries she has two more opportunities to make at least three free throws.

3. The graph shows the results of a simulation of 100 tries of eight free throws each, where the player has a 50% chance of scoring on each free throw.

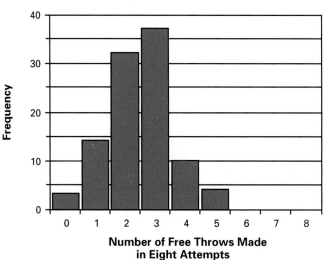

**100 Simulations of
Shooting Free Throws (50% Chance)**

a. Estimate the chance that a player with a 50% chance of scoring a free throw will make three free throws in the next eight tries.

b. Estimate the chance that the player will make at least three free throws in the next eight tries.

c. Is the chance that the player will make at least three free throws in the next eight tries greater than or less than the chance of making less than three? Explain your reasoning.

4. Jesse wrote four statements about chance on the board. Which ones do you think are true and why?

a. The chance of getting H T T T H when you toss a coin is smaller than the chance of getting T H T H T.

b. The chance of getting all heads in five tosses of a coin is the same as the chance of getting all tails.

c. The chance of getting at least six out of ten questions by guessing correctly on a ten-question test is the same as 1 minus the chance of getting up to five questions correct by guessing.

d. If you get a long string of heads in a row when you toss a coin, the chance that you will get a tail next is more than 50%.

Section C. In the Long Run (continued)

3. a. The chance of making exactly three of the free throws in the next eight tries is about $\frac{37}{100}$ or 37%.

b. The chance of making at least three free throws in the next eight tries is $\frac{37 + 10 + 4}{10}$ which is 51%.

c. The chance of making at least three free throws in the next eight tries is a little greater than the chance of making fewer than three free throws. The chance of making at least three free throws is 51%, which is more than 50%. So the chance of making fewer than three is 100%–51%, or 49%.

4. a. Not true: The chances of getting HTTTH and THTHT when tossing a coin are equal. You might suggest that students draw a tree diagram to support their answer. Each of these outcomes is just one route in the tree diagram.

b. True: The chance of getting all heads in five tosses of a coin is the same as the chance of getting all tails, because the chance of tossing heads is equal to the chance of tossing tails.

c. True: The results should be the same value. The chance of getting at least six out of ten questions correct by guessing on a ten question test is the same as 1 minus the chance of getting up to five questions correct by guessing. This is true because one can either have 0, 1, 2, 3, 4, 5, 6, 7, 8, 9, or 10 questions correct by guessing. If you add up the chances of all these outcomes, you get 1. So if you add up all the chances of having at least 6 out of 10 correct (6, 7, 8, 9, or 10), and subtract this from 1; this is the same as the chance of not having 6, 7, 8, 9, or 10 correct (which is also the same as chance of having 0, 1, 2, 3, 4 or 5, or "up to 5 questions correct").

d. Not true: If you get a long string of heads in a row, the chance that you will get a tail on the next toss is still 50%. The coin does not remember the previous results.

◆ Additional Practice

Section Ⓓ Computing Chances

1. All the students in Jamie's school will get a new code of three digits for their lockers. How can you compute, in a smart way, the chance that her code will be 2–5–6?

2. Matthew has a 75% free-throw shooting percentage. He wants to know the chance he has of making both free throws if he takes two shots.

   a. Calculate this chance. Explain how you found your answer.

   b. What is Matthew's chance of missing at least one shot if he takes four shots? Explain how you found your answer.

3. Hillary rides her bike to school. There are two traffic lights on the way. By keeping track of how often the lights are green when she gets to them, she has found out that the first traffic light is green around $\frac{1}{3}$ of the time and the second about $\frac{1}{4}$ of the time.

   She makes the following chance tree to compute the chance that she has to stop twice on her way to school.

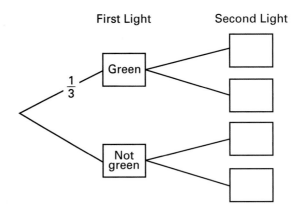

   a. Finish the chance tree.

   b. What is the chance that she has to stop twice on her way to school?

   c. What is the chance that she has to stop only once?

   d. Draw an area model for the problem of the two traffic lights.

Section D. Computing Chances

1. You compute the chance that Jamie's code will be 2–5–6 by making a chance tree or by reasoning and calculating. This is part of the chance tree:

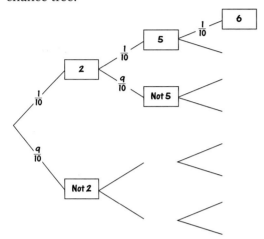

So the chance of having code 2–5–6 is

$\frac{1}{10} \times \frac{1}{10} \times \frac{1}{10} = \frac{1}{1000}$ or 0.1%

2. a. The chance of making both shots is indicated by the large square on the bottom left, which is $\frac{3}{4} \times \frac{3}{4} = \frac{9}{16}$, which is about 56%. Comment: Instead of using an area model, this problem can also be solved by making a chance tree.

First shot

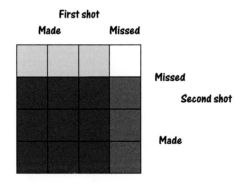

b. Matthew's chance of missing at least one shot if he takes four shots can be found with a chance tree or by reasoning. Note: This is not the same as the chance that Matthew misses **exactly** one shot.

When computing the chance that Matthew misses **at least** one shot, you need to take into account the chance that he misses 1, 2, 3, or all four shots. In this case, it would be best to use complementary chances: that is,

the chance that Matthew misses at least one of four shots is 1 minus the chance that he doesn't miss any shot (or makes all four). The chance that Matthew will make all four shots is $\frac{3}{4} \times \frac{3}{4} \times \frac{3}{4} \times \frac{3}{4}$, or about 32%. So the chance that he misses at least one free throw is 100% – 32%, which is 68%.

3. a.

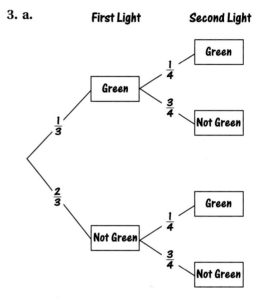

b. If Hillary has to stop twice on her way to school, this means both lights are "not green." The chance of this happening is $\frac{2}{3} \times \frac{3}{4} = \frac{6}{12}$, or 50% of the time.

c. Hillary has to stop only once when she encounters two sequences: "not green"–"green", or "green"–"not green." The chance for the not green-green path is $\frac{2}{3} \times \frac{1}{4} = \frac{2}{12}$. The chance for the green–not green path is $\frac{1}{3} \times \frac{3}{4} = \frac{3}{12}$. Together the chance to stop only once is $\frac{2}{12} + \frac{3}{12} = \frac{5}{12}$.

d.

First Light

Not Green   Green

Green

Second Light

Not Green

Assessment Overview

Unit assessments in *Mathematics in Context* include two quizzes and a Unit Test. Quiz 1 is to be used anytime after students have completed Section B. Quiz 2 can be used after students have completed Section C. The Unit Test addresses many of the major goals of the unit. You can evaluate student responses to these assessments to determine what each student knows about the content goals addressed in this unit.

Pacing

Each quiz is designed to take approximately 25 minutes to complete. The unit test is designed to be completed during a 45-minute class period. For more information on how to use these assessments, see the Planning Assessment section on the next page.

Goals	Assessment Opportunities		Problem Levels
• Use counting strategies, trees, two-way tables, and rules to find probability.	Quiz 1 Quiz 2 Test	Problems 3abc Problems 4de Problems 2abc, 3abc, 4c, 5ac	
• Use different representations (ratios, percents, fractions, and so on) to describe probability.	Quiz 2	Problems 1, 3a, 4bc	I
• Use complementary probability to determine the chance for an event.	Test	Problem 2d	
• Find the possible outcomes for various situations, games, and experiments.	Quiz 1 Quiz 2 Test	Problems 1ab, 4a Problem 1 Problems 1ab, 4abc	
• Use simulation and modeling to investigate probability.	Quiz 1 Quiz 2 Test	Problem 4b Problems 2, 3c Problems 4bc	
• Make decisions using probability and expected values.	Quiz 2	Problems 3b, 4a	II
• Understand the limitations of and relationship between various models used to find probability.	Quiz 1 Quiz 2 Test	Problem 2 Problem 2 Problems 2d, 3d	
• Understand that variability is inherent in any probability situation.	Quiz 2	Problem 3c	
• Develop a critical attitude toward the use of probability.	Test	Problem 5b	III

About the Mathematics

These assessment activities assess the majority of the goals for *Second Chance*. Refer to the Goals and Assessment Opportunities section on the previous page for information regarding the goals that are assessed in each problem. Some of the problems that involve multiple skills and processes address more than one unit goal. To assess students' ability to engage in non-routine problem solving (a Level III goal in the Assessment Pyramid), some problems assess students' ability to use their skills and conceptual knowledge in new situations. For example, in the street lights problem on the Unit Test (problem 5b), students need to critically analyze a false proposition regarding probability for a new problem context.

Planning Assessment

These assessments are designed for individual assessment; however, some problems can be done in pairs or small groups. It is important that students work individually if you want to evaluate each student's understanding and abilities.

Make sure you allow enough time for students to complete the problems. If students need more than one class session to complete the problems, it is suggested that they finish during the next mathematics class, or you may assign select problems as a take-home activity. Students should be free to solve the problems their own way. Student use of calculators is at the teachers' discretion.

If individual students have difficulties with any particular problems, you may give the student the option of making a second attempt after providing him or her a hint. You may also decide to use one of the optional problems or Extension activities not previously done in class as additional assessments for students who need additional help.

Scoring

Solution and scoring guides are included for each quiz and the Unit Test. The method of scoring depends on the types of questions on each assessment. A holistic scoring approach could also be used to evaluate an entire quiz.

Several problems require students to explain their reasoning or justify their answers. For these questions, the reasoning used by students in solving the problems as well as the correctness of the answers should be considered in your scoring and grading scheme.

Student progress toward goals of the unit should be considered when reviewing student work. Descriptive statements and specific feedback are often more informative to students than a total score or grade. You might choose to record descriptive statements of select aspects of student work as evidence of student progress toward specific goals of the unit that you have identified as essential.

Second Chance Quiz 1

Use additional paper as needed.

1. The breakfast menu at Kelly's Place has a choice of cereal, eggs, or French toast. The drink choices are milk, juice, or coffee.

   a. How many different breakfast combinations are possible? Make a tree diagram.

   b. Fran only drinks juice or coffee for breakfast, and she never eats eggs. How many possible combinations does she have to choose from?

2. Carol's mom and Andrew's mom are each going to have a baby. Carol has two sisters, and Andrew has a brother and a sister. Carol says to Andrew, "My mom has a greater chance of having a boy than yours does." Do you agree or disagree with Carol? Explain your reasoning.

3. Robert and Hillary surveyed all of the students in grades 7 and 8 to find out whether or not they wear glasses.

	Boy	Girl	Total
Glasses	15	20	
No Glasses			
Total	53		100

   a. Complete the rest of the table.

   b. If you randomly select a student, what is the chance this student wears glasses?

   c. If you were told the student selected in part **b** must be a boy, what would be the chance the student selected wears glasses?

4. In the game of CAT, three coins are flipped. Player A gets a point if two heads and a tail come up. If they don't come up, player B gets a point.

   a. Make a list of possible outcomes for flipping three coins. Choose your own way to display the various outcomes. How many possible outcomes are there?

   b. Do you think this is a fair game? Explain why or why not.

Use additional paper as needed.

1. If you roll a number cube one hundred times, about how many times do you expect an odd number to be rolled? Explain.

2. Describe a chance situation or game for which you cannot compute the chances beforehand. Explain why it is not possible to compute the chances in your example.

3. Some coins have head and tail sides that are very different. These coins cannot be used for a fair simulation. Deborah and Hank have a coin they suspect is unfair, which means the chance of the coin landing on heads or tails is not equal.

   a. If you toss a fair coin, what is the chance of tossing a heads or tails? Express the chance as a fraction as well as a percent.

   b. Deborah and Hank tossed their coin 200 times. They tossed heads 80 times, and they tossed tails 120 times. Can they conclude now that the coin is not fair?

c. Deborah and Hank repeated their experiment many times. The table shows their results.

Experiment Number	Number of Heads in 200 Tosses	Number of Tails in 200 Tosses
1	80	120
2	84	116
3	97	103
4	98	102
5	94	106
6	91	109
7	77	123
8	92	108
9	101	99
10	95	105

After reviewing the results of these ten experiments, what is your conclusion? Be sure to explain how you came to this conclusion.

4. Daniel and Kirk are members of the darts team at their schools. Daniel's team consists of five students, and Kirk's team consists of 4 students. All of the students have about the same level of competency in dart throwing. Only two students from each team will be selected as representatives for the local darts tournament. Team members must be selected randomly.

a. What does "selected randomly" mean in this situation?

Use additional paper as needed.

b. What is the chance that Daniel will be selected for the tournament? Express this chance as a fraction.

c. What is the chance that Kirk will be selected for the tournament? Express this chance as a fraction.

d. Use an area model to find the chance that both Daniel and Kirk will be chosen for the tournament.

e. What is the chance that neither Daniel nor Kirk will be chosen for the tournament?

1. Joan has laid out some of her clothes. There are 3 pairs of pants, 4 shirts, and two pairs of shoes (tennis shoes and dress shoes). She cannot decide what to wear. She sighs, "Oh! I can make at least 20 different outfits, but I cannot decide which one to wear!"

   a. Is it true that Joan can make at least 20 different outfits with the clothes she laid out? Show how you found your answer.

   b. Joan decides to wear her tennis shoes. How many outfits can she choose from now?

Use additional paper as needed.

2. A survey was given to 1,000 customers to find out the type of movie they purchased on DVD. The graph displays the survey data. Use this graph to answer the questions below.

Percentage of DVDs Sold by Catagory

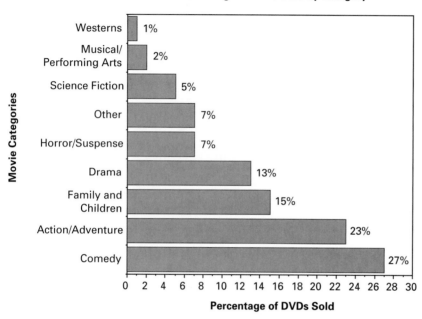

a. Of the people surveyed, how many purchased an action/adventure DVD?

b. Suppose one of the surveyed customers was selected at random. What is the chance that this customer purchased a science fiction DVD?

c. What is the chance that a customer from the survey bought a DVD that is not a comedy?

d. What can you say about the chance that a randomly selected customer from the sample bought a comedy DVD and the chance that the customer did not buy a comedy DVD?

3. A survey was given to 150 seventh grade students at Bell Middle School. Here are some of the results.

- 62 of the students played video games 2 or more hours a day.
- 45 of the students played video games 2 or more hours a day and liked school.
- The chance that a random chosen student likes school is $\frac{2}{3}$.

	Like School	Do Not Like School	Total
Play Video Games 2 or More Hours a Day			
Play Video Games Less Than 2 Hours a Day			
Total			

a. Complete the table using the information from the survey.

b. What is the chance that a randomly chosen seventh grade student plays video games less than 2 hours a day and likes school?

c. If you know that a student likes school, what is the chance that the student plays video games less than 2 hours a day?

d. What is the difference between problems 3b and 3c?

4. Howard and Rudolf play a game rolling three number cubes. If the sum of the three number cubes is an even number, Howard wins. If the sum of the three number cubes is odd, Rudolf wins.

a. Do you think this a fair game? Explain your answer.

Use additional paper as needed.

Howard and Rudolf had a computer simulate rolling three number cubes 500 times. The results are displayed in the graph below.

Sum	3	4	5	6	7	8	9	10	11	12	13	14	15	16	17	18
Number	3	10	13	24	32	55	53	57	59	58	52	36	28	11	8	1

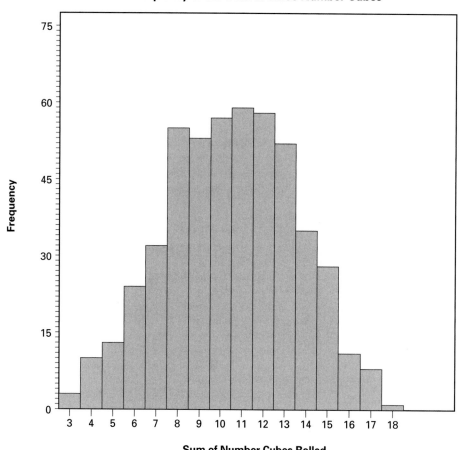

Frequency of the Sum of Three Number Cubes

Sum of Number Cubes Rolled

b. Given the results from this computer simulation, do you want to change your answer to problem 4a? Use the information from the graph to support your answer.

c. What is the largest sum you can roll using three number cubes? Calculate the chance on this outcome. Show your work.

5. Ann bikes to school every morning. She passes two traffic lights. The chance that she has to stop for the first one is 0.4, the chance that she has to stop for the second one is 0.7.

   a. What is the chance that Ann has to stop for both lights? Show your work.

   Ann's brother, Bobby, thinks that the chance that Ann does not have to stop for either light is $\frac{1}{3}$. He reasons, "Ann has to stop for either two lights, one light, or no lights. So there are three possibilities, and the chance for each is 1 out of 3. This is $\frac{1}{3}$."

   b. Explain why Bobby is wrong.

   c. Use a tree diagram or a chance tree to calculate the chance that Ann has to stop for only one of the lights.

Second Chance Quiz 1
Solution and Scoring Guide

Possible student answer	Suggested number of score points	Problem level
1. a. There are 9 different combinations. cereal — milk, juice, coffee eggs — milk, juice, coffee French toast — milk, juice, coffee	**2** (Award 1 point for a correct answer, 1 point for a correct tree diagram.)	I
b. Fran has now 4 choices.	1	I
2. I do not agree with Carol. The chance for a boy or girl to be born does not depend on previous births, just as throwing a 6 with a number cube does not depend on earlier throws. (This response assumes that Carol's parents have an equal chance of having a boy or a girl. In fact, historical trends show that the chance of having a boy or girl is not 50/50. The chance of having a boy is slightly more than the chance of having a girl, 51% to 49%).	2	II
3. a.	**3** (Subtract 1 point for any missing or incorrect answer until 0 score points are reached.)	I
b. 35 students out of 100 wear glasses; or $\frac{35}{100}$, or 35%	1	I
c. The chance would now be 15 out of 53, which is about 28%, since you only have to look at the boys.	1	I

Table for 3. a.:

	Boy	Girl	Total
Glasses	15	20	35
No Glasses	38	27	65
Total	53	47	100

Possible student answer	Suggested number of score points	Problem level
4. a. Note that students may choose their own representation. Sample list of all possibilities: HHH HHT HTH HTT THH THT TTH TTT (There are 8 different possible outcomes.)	3	I
b. The game is *not* fair. Player A gets a point for 3 out of 8 combinations, and player B gets a point for 5 out of 8 combinations. Player B has a better chance to win.	3 (Award 2 points for a correct explanation, 1 point for a correct conclusion.)	II
Total score points	16	

Second Chance Quiz 2
Solution and Scoring Guide

Possible student answer	Suggested number of score points	Problem level
1. About 50 times. Sample explanation: There are 3 odd numbers and 3 even numbers on a number cube. The chance that an odd number will be rolled is 3 out of 6, or $\frac{1}{2}$, or 50%.	**2** (Award 1 point for a correct answer, 1 point for a correct explanation.)	I
2. Sample situation: Throw a pushpin and find the chance that it will land on the pin's head with the point up. You cannot compute the chance for this situation because a pushpin is not a regularly shaped or symmetrical object. The chance to land "point up" is certainly not 50%. I expect the pushpin will land "point up" only a few number of times.	**2** (Award 1 point for a correct situation, 1 point for a correct explanation.)	II
3. a. $\frac{1}{2}$, or 50%	**1**	I
b. No, this was only one experiment. This result may be due to variability. However, since 200 is a large number of trials, it is likely that the coin may be unfair.	**2** (Award 1 for "no," 1 for the explanation.)	II
c. Sample conclusion: In most of the experiments, heads and tails are tossed close to 100 each time. So the coin may be fair. However, in 9 of the 10 experiments, the number of heads tossed is smaller than the number of tails tossed. If you add up all numbers, 909 out of 2,000 tosses are heads: this is 45%. For this reason, it seems that the coin is not fair, and favors tails."	**2**	II/III

Possible student answer	Suggested number of score points	Problem level
4. a. Each student has an equal chance of being selected for the tournament. One student is not favored over another.	1	I/II
b. $\frac{2}{5}$	1	I
c. $\frac{2}{4}$ or $\frac{1}{2}$	1	I
d. $\frac{1}{5}$ 4 out of 20, or $\frac{4}{20}$, which is $\frac{1}{5}$.	3 (Award 1 point for a correct answer, 2 points for a correct model.)	I
e. $\frac{3}{5} \times \frac{1}{2} = \frac{3}{10}$	1	I
Total score points	16	

Second Chance Unit Test
Solution and Scoring Guide

Possible student answers	Suggested number of score points	Problem level
1. a. Yes, it is true. Joan can make 24 different outcomes. Strategies may vary: • using a tree diagram • drawing or listing all outfits • using multiplication 3 × 4 × 2	**3** (Award 1 point for a correct answer, 2 points for a correct strategy)	I
b. She can chose from 12 outfits now. Sample reasoning: Each of 3 pants can be combined with 4 different shirts.	2	I
2. a. 230 people. 0.23 × 1,000 people surveyed = 230	2	I
b. 5%	2	I
c. 73% The chance that someone purchased a comedy DVD is 27%. So the chance that someone purchased a DVD that is not a comedy is 100% − 27% = 73%.	2	I
d. Student responses should demonstrate the concept of "complementary chances." Sample responses: • These chances add up to 100%. • Chances together are 1. • If you know one of these chances, you can find the other by subtracting it from 100%. • These chances are complementary.	2	I/II
3. a.	**3** (Award 1 point for correctly filling in the 62, 45 and 150, 1 point for 100 and 50 in the last row, and 1 point for the other numbers.)	I

3. a.

	Like School	Do Not Like School	Total
Play Video Games 2 or More Hours a Day	45	17	62
Play Video Games Less Than 2 Hours a Day	55	33	88
Total	100	50	150

Possible student answers	Suggested number of score points	Problem level
b. 55 out of 150, or $\frac{55}{150}$, or $\frac{11}{30}$, or "about 37%"	1	I
c. 55 out of 100, or $\frac{55}{100}$, or 55%	1	I
d. Sample answer: In **3b** you consider the total number of students, whereas in **3c** you only look at the group who likes school.	2	II

Possible student answers	Suggested number of score points	Problem level
4. a. Yes, this is fair game. Sample explanation: With three number cubes, you may roll any sum from 3 through 18. There are as many ways to roll an even sum as there are to roll an odd sum.	**2** (Award 1 point for the answer, 1 point for a correct explanation.)	I
b. Accept an answer of *No* or *Yes*, depending on responses to **4a**. Sample explanations: • The game is fair because the graph is almost symmetric, so the chance of rolling 3 is the same as rolling 18. The chance of rolling a 4 is the same as rolling a 17, and so on. So the chance of rolling an even sum is the same as rolling an odd sum. • I added the number of times an even number came up on the graph, and this was about 250. So the chance is about 50%, and the game is fair.	**2**	I/II
c. The largest sum is 18. The chance for rolling 18 is 1 out of 216 (6 × 6 × 6). Sample calculation: Using a chance tree, the chance of rolling a 6 with one number cube is $\frac{1}{6}$; each branch has a chance of $\frac{1}{6}$, so the chance on a sum of 18 is $\frac{1}{6} \times \frac{1}{6} \times \frac{1}{6} = \frac{1}{216}$.	**3** (Award partial credit if students use the results from the simulation to determine that the chance for rolling 18 is $\frac{1}{500}$.) (Award 2 points for the answers, 1 point for correct student work.)	I/II
5. a. 0.28 or 28% Students can find their answer using a chance tree, an area diagram, or by calculating 0.4 × 0.7.	**3** (Award 1 point for the answer, 2 points for correct student work.)	I
b. Sample explanations: • Bobby is wrong. There are 3 possibilities but they do not all have the same chance. • Bobby is wrong. If I calculate the chance, it is 0.6 × 0.3 = 0.18, which is less than $\frac{1}{3}$.	**2** (Award 1 point for the correct answer, 2 points for correct student work.)	III

Possible student answer	Suggested number of score points	Problem level
c. 0.54 or 54% Sample calculation using a chance tree: The chance is: 0.4 × 0.3 + 0.6 × 0.7 = 0.12 + 0.42 = 0.54 or 54%	3	I
Total score points	35	

Chance tree:

- 0.4 → Wait
  - 0.7 → Wait
  - 0.3 → Drive
- 0.6 → Drive
  - 0.7 → Wait
  - 0.3 → Drive

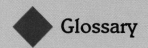
Glossary

The Glossary defines all vocabulary words indicated in this unit. It includes the mathematical terms that may be new to students, as well as words having to do with the contexts introduced in the unit. (Note: The Student Book has no Glossary in order to allow students to construct their own definitions, based on their personal experiences with the unit activities.)

The definitions below are specific for the use of the terms in this unit. The page numbers given are from the Student Book.

area model (p. 39) a rectangular model to find the chance that two combined events will occur

chance or probability (p. 1, 14) the possibility that an event will occur

chance tree (p. 37) a tree diagram with branches representing the chance that an event is expected to occur

combined events (p. 35) a sequence of events or events occurring simultaneously

experimental chance (p. 14) or (estimated) chance; the experimental or empirical probability of an event to occur

frequency (p. 13) the number of times an event occurs

random selection (TG p. 15T) a sample chosen from a population in such a way that everyone in the population has an equal chance of being selected for the sample

simulation (p. 29)   an imitation to model an experiment

theoretical chance (p. 20T) the (calculated) chance that an event may be expected to occur, found without collecting data

tree diagram (p. 2) a picture with branches representing all possible outcomes or combinations of outcomes

trial (p. 32T) one of many repetitions of an experiment or simulation

two-way table (p. 17) a table used to structure and record information on two related events

BRITANNICA

Mathematics
in
Context

Blackline
Masters

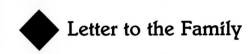

Dear Family,

Soon your child will be starting the *Mathematics in Context* unit *Second Chance*. Below is a letter to your child that opens the unit, describing the unit and its goals.

You can help your child relate the class work to his or her own life by asking for help in making fair decisions at home by flipping a coin, rolling a number cube, or picking straws. As part of the decision-making process, have your child figure out the probability of guessing the toss of the coin or roll of the dice or picking the correct straw.

Look for other opportunities to bring chance and probability into the home, such as probabilities used with weather reports, sports statistics, and board games. If you have games that use number cubes or spinners, discuss how chance is involved in each game. Do the games seem to be fair?

Check newspapers for statements about chance and read them to your child. Chance is an important concept in dealing with uncertainty and is a factor in many situations, such as determining insurance rates, making predictions, and studying risk.

We hope you enjoy working with your child as he or she explores games and situations involving chance.

Sincerely,

The Mathematics in Context Development Team

Dear Student

One thing is for sure: Our lives are full of uncertainty. We are not certain what the weather tomorrow will be or if we are going to win a game. Perhaps the game is not even fair!

In this unit you learn to count possibilities in smart ways and to do experiments about chance. You will also simulate and compute chances. What is the chance that a family with four children has four girls? How likely is it that the next child in the family will be another girl? You will learn to adjust the scoring for games to make them fair.

Sometimes information from surveys can be recorded in tables and used to make chance statements.

Chance is one way to help us measure uncertainty. Chance plays a role in decisions that we make and what we do in our lives! It is important to understand how chance works!

We hope you enjoy the unit!

Sincerely,

The Mathematics in Context Development Team

Name _____

Student Activity Sheet 1
Use with *Second Chance*, pages 2 and 3.

Trip

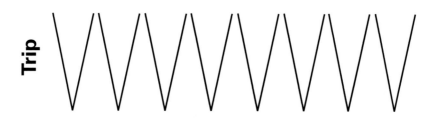

Accomodation

Lakes

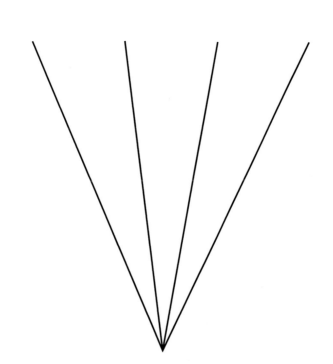

Student Activity Sheet 2
Use with *Second Chance*, pages 6 and 7.

Name _____

	1	2	3	4	5	6
1	1 1	1 2	1 3	1 4	1 5	1 6
2	2 1	2 2	2 3	2 4	2 5	2 6
3	3 1	3 2	3 3	3 4	3 5	3 6
4	4 1	(4 2)	4 3	4 4	4 5	4 6
5	5 1	5 2	5 3	5 4	5 5	5 6
6	6 1	6 2	6 3	6 4	6 5	6 6

Sum of rolling two number cubes

Sum (+)	1	2	3	4	5	6
1	2					
2						
3				7		
4		6				
5						
6					11	

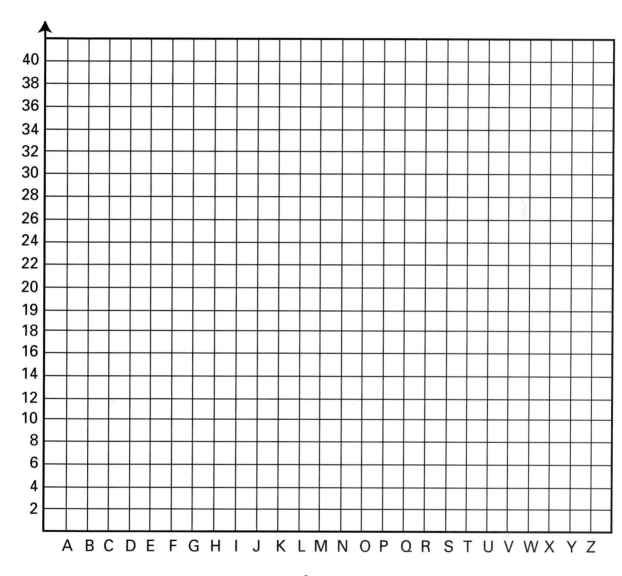

◆ **Student Activity Sheet 3b**
Use with *Second Chance*, page 14.

Name _____

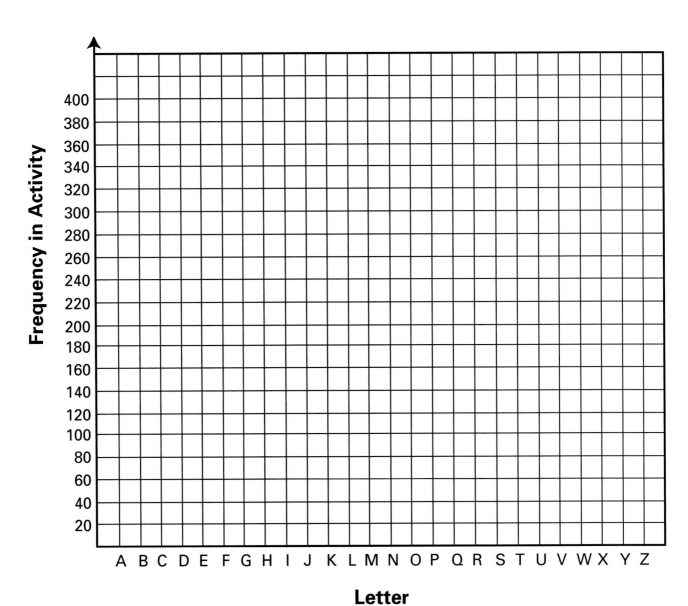

Name _____

Student Activity Sheet 4
Use with *Second Chance*, page 24.

Ratio of Number of Heads to Total Number of Tosses of a Coin

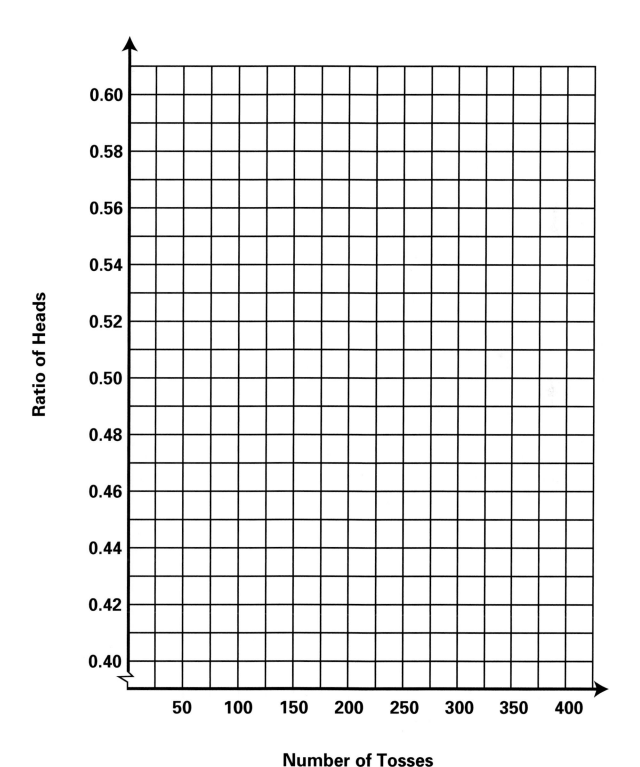

Ratio of Heads

0.60
0.58
0.56
0.54
0.52
0.50
0.48
0.46
0.44
0.42
0.40

50   100   150   200   250   300   350   400

Number of Tosses

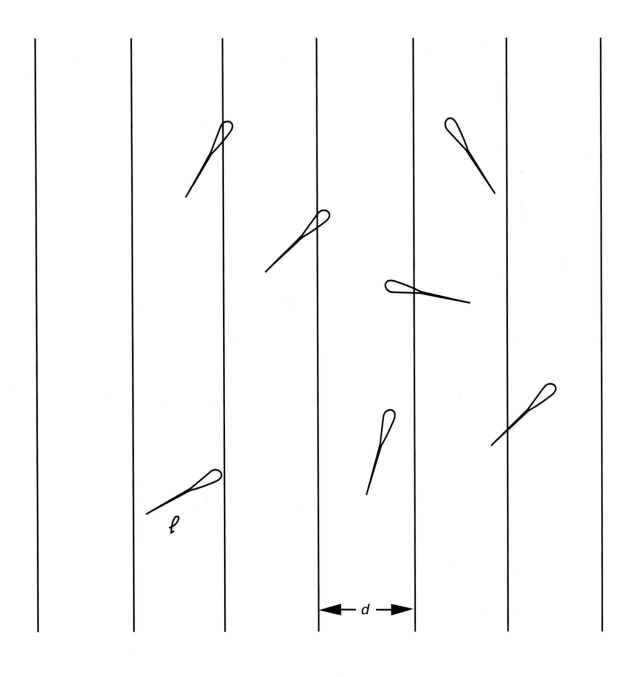

The results are in the table.

2. a. By looking at the results in the table can you tell who is right—Janet or Karji? Explain.

    b. Which chance do you think is bigger—that the first car leaving the parking lot is red or that the first car leaving the lot is white? Why?

Color	Number of Cars
Red	13
White	24
Other	63
Total	**100**

As a class, you are going to investigate car colors in a parking lot or on the street.

First agree on six colors you want to record. Record cars that are not one of those six colors as "other."

Design a form on which you can record the car colors.

Record the colors of 25 different cars. Try to choose a different set of cars from ones chosen by others in your class.

3. a. Combine the class results in one table. Make a graph of the results.

    b. Calculate the percentage of cars in each color.

Suppose all of the cars the class tallied in the activity were from the same parking lot.

4. a. Which color car are you most likely to see leaving the parking lot?

    b. Is it possible that the first car entering the parking lot the day after you counted colors is a color that you did not record in the activity? Explain your answer.

    c. Write three statements involving chance based on your findings about car colors.

Hints and Comments
(continued from page 11T)

About the Mathematics

Systematic data collection can provide information about possible outcomes, their relative frequency, and experimental probabilities. If there is a need to have reliable chance statements to make decisions for a large population or future events, the information must be data collected from a large enough representative sample or for a comparable event. Otherwise, chance statements are only reliable for the sample that was surveyed. In the case of the car color activity, the sample students collect data from will not be representative for all cars. So the chance statements will only be reliable for the cars in the sample or for the cars on the parking lot where the sample was taken.

Planning

Students can work in small groups on problem 2 and discuss the answers in class. Prepare the activity as a whole class. If this is completed as a class activity, instead of having each student record the colors of 25 cars, have them work in pairs or small groups. You may need about one lesson to collect and record the data, depending on where students need to go to collect the data. Problem 3a is a whole class activity. Students may work on problems 3b and 4 in small groups and discuss answers to problem 4.

Comments About the Solutions

2. Discuss answers in class. Answers are acceptable as long as student explanations are reasonable. Note that the first two sample answers given in this Teacher's Guide have to do with the numbers in the table (results from data collection), while the second two sample answers have to do with the way the sample was chosen. Try to make sure both types of reasoning are included in the class discussion.

Activity

Take a newspaper article or a text from any book. With a classmate, record the first 100 letters in this text in a frequency table.

9. Use **Student Activity Sheet 3a** to make a graph of the frequencies for each letter.

10. **a.** What is the most common letter in your selection? Was this the same for every pair of students in your class?

   b. Compare your graph with your classmates' graphs. What do you notice?

11. **a.** On **Student Activity Sheet 3b**, combine the letter frequency graphs you made in problem 9 into one class graph.

   b. Write three lines comparing the graph to the letter frequency table.

The results of an experiment or data collection can be used to estimate the chance an event will occur. Chances found this way are called **experimental chances**.

12. Use the data in your frequency table from problem 11 to answer the following:

   a. If you close your eyes and select a letter from a newspaper, estimate the chance that you pick an O.

   b. As a class, compare your answers in part **a** by making a dot plot on the number line of the estimated chances. Use the plot to help you write a sentence about the probability of selecting the letter O from a newspaper with your eyes closed.

   c. Estimate the chance of picking three other letters. Choose one with a high probability of being picked and another with a low probability of being picked. The third one can be any letter you want. Write each answer as a fraction and as a decimal.

Hints and Comments
(continued from page 14T)

Overview

Students record the frequency of 100 letters from a selected text. They graph the results of their sample text and the results for the whole class. They write chance statements based on the results and compare these to the percentages in the letter frequency table on page 13.

About the Mathematics

The relative frequency of a letter can be interpreted as the chance of picking that letter "in the future." Of course, these chances are only reliable for other texts if the sample on which the frequencies are based is large enough and representative of English texts.

Planning

Have students complete the activity and problems 9, 10, 11b, and 12 in pairs. If there is enough time, student pairs can complete the analysis of two different texts of 100 letters. Complete problem 11a as a whole class activity.

Comments About the Solutions

10. b. Stack the sheets with graphs on top of each other. Hold them in front of a light or against a window to see if the patterns match.

11. a. If the sample is large enough and the texts that were chosen are representative, the frequencies in the graph should be close to those in the table on page 13. Note that the class graph shows the absolute frequencies, but the order will be about the same as those of the relative frequencies in the table.